Letters to My Patients

Letters to My Patients

A guide to healthy
and happy living.

Harlan O. L. Wright, D.O.

Shallowater Press
P.O. Box 1151
Shallowater, Texas 79363

Shallowater Press
P.O. Box 1151
Shallowater, TX 79363-1151

Printed and bound in the United States of America.

First printing October 1995.

ISBN 0-9648404-0-5

Library of Congress Catalog Card Number: 95-74719

Publisher: Todd Knowlton
Developmental Editors: Todd Knowlton, Melissa Knowlton
Copy Editor: Dawna Walls
Cover Design: Kip Kubisz
Cover Art: Bryan Dudley
Cover Photo and Text: Laura Story Melton

Acknowledgments

I would be remiss if I didn't give ample thanks and credit to those who have encouraged me for the past several years to put some of my unique healing methods down on paper. My wife, Lynne, has expressed the thought for a long time that I should record some of the knowledge that I have acquired over the years for the benefit of our children and grandchildren. She has also been very instrumental in making suggestions and editorial criticism.

My children and in-law children have been a constant source of support and encouragement.

My nurse Liz, and my receptionist Janis, who have worked with me for more than ten years, want the book badly so they won't have to continually make back copies of my newsletters for patients who have missed some.

Untold numbers of my patients have encouraged me to try to train someone to do the work that I am doing and if that is not possible, to at least put some of this health assistance in a book. I suspect they are worried that I might retire and leave them in need.

Last but foremost, I thank my granddaughter, Laura Story Melton, who has been a constant source of encouragement and enthusiasm and who has done most of the editing. Without her help, the information in this book would probably never have gotten to a publisher.

Preface

This book is unique in that it teaches not only valuable lessons on the attainment of health but also expresses my philosophy of life developed through seventy-four years of experience.

The chapters in this book were originally written as monthly "Letters to My Patients." Each letter was on a different subject which I believed would be of interest and educational value to my patients. Each letter contained a prologue which, while not necessarily directly related to the medical material of the letter, enhanced its value with a philosophy which I believe to be very important to the attainment of optimum health and enjoyment of living.

The format of the original letters has been changed as necessary to accommodate the publishing of the book, but the material remains basically the same.

I do essentially all of my writing from my little mountain home in Alto, New Mexico. I have always loved the mountains, and for many years a mountain home with a panoramic view had been my dream. Therefore, you will see frequent references to "my little bit of heaven" or "sitting on the deck" or comments about the mountain beauty. The "mountain" is the 12,000 ft. Sierra Blanca peak in the Sacramento Mountain Range.

Contents

Introduction

In the eyes of the general population in this country, I am considered an old man—an old doctor. Although I am seventy-four years of age and have practiced medicine for the past forty-three years, I don't feel old. In fact, I probably feel better today than I did when I was fifty because I have changed my lifestyle a great deal in the past twenty-five years or so. I still work eight to ten hours a day, get a lot of exercise playing tournament tennis, don't take medications of any kind, have no aches or pains, and have no physical impairments or diseases. In the process of being able to accomplish these things, I must be doing something right.

The genetics on my father's side of the family dictate that I should have been dead fourteen or more years ago. All the male members of my family were dead of heart attacks by the age of sixty. Although genetics play a definite role in our health tendencies, many of those genetic disadvantages can be overcome by close attention to our lifestyle.

During the past twenty-five years or so, I have become increasingly aware of the tremendous healing power of nutritional therapy. I have become convinced that optimum health is attainable only if we treat our bodies with respect and nourish them with the elements nature intended. If we don't, we must "pay the piper" and the results of that payment can readily be seen in the tremendous amount of money this nation spends on disease care—*not health care*—every year! It is ironic that our government gives so much lip service to preventive medicine and health care when what is really being practiced by ninety percent of the "health" practitioners in this country is only disease care—treatment of conditions which could be largely prevented by true health care. Medical orthodoxy still looks for miracle drugs and spectacular surgical procedures to impart health. They are, of course, barking up a very profitable tree. However, I believe that their premise is sadly misguided. If even a small portion of the billions of dollars spent each year on illness and disease was spent educating people on true lifestyles of health, I sincerely believe that much more than half of the total cost of illness could be saved.

No one realizes better than I that poor lifestyle habits formed from babyhood are hard to change. They can be changed only if one realizes that these habits are detrimental to health. The incentive must be present to open your mind to the realization that changing these detrimental habits will give you a more enjoyable and vigorous life, relatively free from anxiety, depression, and physical discomfort. We have been brainwashed by constant exposure to the advertising of hospitals, doctors and the pharmaceutical industry into thinking that infirmity and physical debility are "normal" as we grow older. If only I can find the words to dispel such acceptance from your mind and forever inoculate you against this erroneous type of negative thinking!

As an osteopathic physician, I am proud to display the degree D.O. instead of the other medical degree M.D. The principles of osteopathy teach that the body has within itself the ability to cure its own illness if given the proper structural integrity to insure normal and adequate blood supply to the various parts of the body. Inherent in this philosophy is the assumption that the blood supply must be of good nutritional quality. Our profession is unique in that it stresses the use of physical manipulative procedures to correct structural abnormalities that are interfering with the normal functioning of the body. Unfortunately for the patient community, many osteopathic physicians graduating today are not taking the time to utilize the manipulative skills that play such an important part in the healing of the patient.

The concepts of osteopathy were started by Andrew Taylor Still, M.D. about 1865. He became disenchanted with the ineffective drug treatment of that time and formulated a method of treatment quite foreign to the accepted medical philosophy of his day. His success in the treatment of illness became so renowned that people from all over his area of the country began coming to him for treatment. As is generally the case with any new concept, his teachings were rejected by his M.D. colleagues and he was ostracized from the medical community. However, the demand for his services became so great that he started his own school of medicine to teach others his methods.

He called his newborn science osteopathy because it involved the correction of abnormalities of the bony structure of the body ("osteo" meaning bone and "pathy" meaning abnormality or disease) in order to overcome disease. The Osteopathic schools of medicine teach proficiency in structural correction by manipulative procedures as well as pharmacology, physiology, anatomy, surgery, and all of the other sciences taught in allopathic (M.D.) schools. Unfortunately, to the great detriment of the patient, comprehensive courses in Nutritional Therapy are not taught in medical schools.

I have been able to attain a high degree of good health and have been able to teach many of my patients to do the same. Because I realize that my years are necessarily numbered, I feel that I have a responsibility to pass on to others some of the secrets and knowledge that I have acquired over the past half century in this much neglected field of health through proper nutrition.

I do a lot of reading. The other day, I ran across an article the contents of which struck me as being particularly apropos. I do not know the author, but the title of the article was "Passport to Happiness: Things Money Can't Buy." The article began, "I was just thinking... When one is on the other side of 60 and there are far less years ahead than there are behind... How does one determine if it has all been worthwhile?" The author then lists about thirty things which determine a worthwhile life. Among them was, "To have accomplished something worthy of being remembered." It made me stop and think what a limited capacity I have for reaching people who really need help with their health problems. Next in importance to my God and my family come my patients. They have been a very large part of my life for the past forty-three years. Maybe I can be of greater service by putting into writing some of the things I have learned during my practice lifetime. For that reason, I started writing "Letters To My Patients."

When I began writing "Letters To My Patients" in January of 1993, I had no idea that they would become so popular. The demand from my patients and from those who have gotten copies from my patients has been so great that it is almost impossible to keep up with the requests for additional back copies. The idea was then born to compile all of this information into a reference book.

Modern medical science has made some fantastic advances in recent years in the areas of high technological equipment for diagnosis, spectacular surgery and life saving techniques for acute care and accidents, but in my opinion has been a dismal failure in learning how to successfully treat the everyday diseases that plague the majority of mankind. After untold years and billions of dollars spent in so-called "health" research, why is it that there is more cancer today than ever before? Why is it that orthodox medicine still has no help for multiple sclerosis patients? If modern medicine is on the right track, why are millions of people suffering from common disorders such as arthritis, high blood pressure, depression, hypoglycemia, diabetes, panic disorders, rheumatic problems, fatigue syndrome, and just plain old "don't feel good?" Patients are generally offered thousands of dollars worth of high technology diagnostic measures and possibly a diagnosis for which they are given many different kinds of prescriptions. When these don't bring the anticipated results, patients are told that they should see a psychiatrist.

It is my belief that God made the human body to be essentially free from disease if we would only follow the laws of nature as closely as we can. I believe that the body has the power in its natural makeup to heal itself in most cases. Drugs are not natural to the human body, but in some cases they may have to be used temporarily as a "crutch" until the powers of nature's own immunity can be strengthened to the point where the body can take care of itself. The proper task of the physician is to see that these conditions exist.

The true purpose of a physician should be to teach. Physicians should show people what they are doing wrong and teach them how to make the changes in their lifestyle that will bring about the healing process, allowing them to take charge of their own health. In my thinking, if my patients stay well, I have succeeded. If they are sick, I have failed. One of the greatest satisfactions I feel is when a patient comes to me in desperation and leaves me in good health.

I realize that there are genetic factors, individual biochemical peculiarities, personal idiosyncrasies, or just lack of will power or incentive that will not allow some patients to get well. But most people can at least be helped to some extent. There is no magic wand that will give us health. But there are many natural laws, which, if utilized, can bring us back to true health—not just temporary freedom from a particular disease.

In the pages of this book, I have attempted to enlighten you not only about the power of nutritional therapy as I have practiced it with my patients, but also about a positive philosophy of life. I believe this philosophy to be an integral part of the healing process and equally as important as the physical lessons taught in this book. These nutritional and philosophical principles are the same principles I have adopted myself, and I believe they are the reason for my continuing active and vigorous lifestyle.

I am going to try to give you some easy, practical steps to follow, and maybe if I can hold the beacon of hope high enough, you will find the incentive and the faith to try to instill in yourselves the behavior necessary for the attainment of good health. I know that in many cases you may have hoped and been disappointed before. But if you will try once again,

I think you will find that a different approach will bring much different results. It is difficult for me to imagine being alive but not enjoying the most precious thing that God has given us—*life*.

It is my sincere hope that you will find in this book many answers to questions about why you feel the way you do and what you can do about it, written in language that you can understand. Don't just read this book—study it—and you will find that the information contained herein can renew your zest for living.

When I am sitting amidst the spectacular beauty of God's hand, all kinds of thoughts come to me that I would like to share with you. Many of them might, at first reflection, seem to have very little to do with health. But after further deliberation, they seem to be quite apropos. After all, the goal of this book is to help you attain total health.

If you were sitting here beside me at this moment in what I call "my little bit of heaven," surveying the vast beauty that God has given us to enjoy, it would not be difficult for me to convey to you the inspiration that I feel, because you would be able to use your sense of sight to inspire like emotions. Words are poor substitutes for sight, but I keep thinking that there must be words adequate to inspire my patients to understand the meaning of the quintessence of health as it could apply to their lives. I must find the words that will give you the incentive and perseverance to do the things that are necessary to attain it.

Being a doctor for more than forty years has taught me a lot of things. Much of what I have learned is from deliberate observation of my patients to learn the causal relationship between the various factors in their lives and their state of health. I would estimate that during my years of practice, I have seen thousands of patients in a variety of circumstances. If I haven't learned anything from that kind of exposure, it is time for me to "hang up the gloves." I have seen so many very special people and probably just as many others who lacked the confidence in themselves to realize that they were special, too. I have also seen many wonderful people who were wasting a valuable part of their lives and their health because of antagonisms and animosities within themselves which actually harmed their physical health. Did you know that anger, hostility, and negative thinking actually produce measurable amounts of toxins from the endocrine glands which in turn produce adverse chemical effects on the body? Are you also aware that thoughts of harmony, love, peace, and joy produce beneficial chemical substances within the body that promote health? Numerous studies have shown this to be true. I guess that's why it's better to be a lover than a fighter.

There is so much greed, immorality, and obscenity going on in the world around us that we tend to lose sight of the admonitions given us in the Original Book of Instruction for our lives (the Bible) which says—to paraphrase—"As a man thinketh in his heart, so is he" and "A joyous heart is good for the stomach" and "Blame creates wounds, but forgiveness heals them." Grudges only hurt the holder.

1

Refined Sugar: Your Most Injurious Temptation

From the time you are old enough to cry, the process of sugar addiction begins. If you cried between feedings, you were given a bottle of sugar water. As you grew a little older, you were fed strained baby foods loaded with sugar. When you got to be old enough to understand, you were promised candy or a soft drink loaded with sugar as a reward. When you became a teenager, you watched all the television ads which subconsciously buried in your mind the idea that you had to eat certain candy bars or drink certain kinds of soft drinks to have lots of energy and lots of girlfriends or boyfriends. From the time you were little, your mother didn't think she was fulfilling her maternal duty unless she made lots of pies and cakes and cookies for you to eat.

Unfortunately, as an adult you are not immune to the prevailing peer pressure of the society in which you find yourself. In this land of plenty, there is rarely any kind of social or business occasion which does not include something to eat—usually some kind of highly refined sweet food. Think about it. How many times have you been to a reception, a party, or even to a friend's house when you were not offered some form of refreshment in which the principal ingredient was sugar?

In your growing years, you have been so accustomed to eating sugar foods that you don't even stop to consider that such eating behavior could be the very thing that has been making you feel tired or depressed or headachy or just plain "out of gas." So, now you seek the services of a doctor because you begin to realize that the old body (which includes the mind) isn't running very well. However, the doctor may be feeling as bad as you do since he has probably been eating about the same way that you have. Since the expertise of the medical profession is primarily in the field of treatment with drugs, you try one drug and then another, each with its own side effects, and finally become entangled in the "medical merry-go-round" with your hopes of ever feeling good again crushed in despair.

Sugar itself, as contained in natural foods, is not bad. It is the refining of these foods that started our downfall. Of course, the sugar companies don't agree and will tell you that "pure" cane sugar is good for you. Most medical professionals also see no harm in it, so you are never educated to the fact that you are slowly killing yourself with your own teeth!

Sugar is the end product of almost everything we eat. The body metabolizes most of our foods into sugar. Our bodies and brains actually run on sugar. Then, you ask, what's wrong with sugar?

There is nothing wrong with sugar as it is found in its natural form. Foods such as grains, fruits, and vegetables contain the necessary vitamins, minerals, and enzymes to help metabolize their own sugar. When we ingest large quantities of refined sugar that contain absolutely *no* nutrients, the nutrients needed to metabolize that refined sugar have to be stolen from the body's reserves. If this process continues long enough, the body becomes deficient in the very things that make it feel good, have plenty of energy, and keep it free from disease.

If you have been in my office, you cannot help but see the sugar cube charts that are hanging on the walls of the treating rooms. Most of the "junk" foods we eat contain lots of refined sugar and not much of anything else. Hence the bad nutritional habits that people form in their earlier years lead to the consumption of tremendous quantities of refined sugar. It takes an amazingly small quantity of sugar to fuel the human body. Did you know that to maintain good health and energy it takes only two or three teaspoons of sugar circulating in the approximately ten pints of blood in your body? Now consider for a moment what an insult it is to your body when you ingest forty or fifty teaspoons of sugar in a day, which isn't at all unusual—eight in each soft drink, twenty-five in each banana split, and fifteen in each piece of chocolate cake. It doesn't take long to add up. Eventually, the body throws up its hands in despair and disease.

Statistics show that the average person in this country eats more than 120 lbs. of sugar a year! The average adult drinks about 30 gallons of soft drinks a year. The average adolescent drinks about 80 gallons of soft drinks a year. It is interesting to note that the average *delinquent* adolescent drinks about 115 gallons per year. That translates into more than 100 lbs. of sugar in just soft drinks alone. That amount is easily doubled by all of the other sweet junk foods ingested! Think about this! *Now don't tell me that refined sugar doesn't mess up your brain!*

You might get the impression that I think refined sugar is the only thing that causes disease. Far from it. There are many other things that contribute to poor health, but you will have to read on to learn more. Hopefully, you will start now with the basics and eliminate refined sugar from your diet as much as possible. It will pay you big dividends, and it won't take long to notice that your body is thanking you.

Last night I awoke at about 4:30 in the morning. It was so light outside that I thought I must have left a light on. I went out to check. There were no lights on, but the sight that I beheld was so enthralling that even though the temperature was about 15 degrees, I had to stand on the deck and marvel at what I was seeing. A three-quarter moon was so bright that only a few stars were visible in an otherwise perfectly clear sky. The reflection of the moon's brightness on the snow-covered mountain allowed me a perfect view of some of God's most beautiful creation. How much beauty He has made for us to enjoy and how little time we take to thank Him for it or to appreciate it. I cannot help but wonder how much physical illness is caused by negative thoughts in whatever form they reveal themselves. How much better it would be to express positive thoughts and appreciation for the many blessings that we constantly enjoy.

As I have told you before, the role of the physician should be that of a teacher. That is the reason I started writing these "Letters To My Patients." In more than forty years of practice I have learned from experience a lot of practical things that make the human body a healthier machine. I feel it is my obligation to pass these things on to my patients, in so far as possible, so that they can experience the same freedom from pain and malady and feel the same joy of living that I do. In order for me to help you, you must first have some understanding of what your problems are, what caused them, and what the treatment prescribed is expected to accomplish—and why. You must enter into the treatment as a partner, with some understanding of our goals and how to attain them. This is my job. This is why the role of the physician as a teacher is so important. This is also the very reason the present medical system is the fastest growing, failing *business in America! How often have you gone into a doctor's office with what to you was a serious problem only to be given a prescription with little or no explanation or apparent interest and to again be disappointed in the results? The physician has failed to adequately perform his or her function.*

2

Aspartame: Another Injurious Temptation

The previous chapter has, I am sure, stopped you from eating most of your sugar-laden foods—or am I dreaming? So now you have switched to that wonderful, calorie-free, great-tasting aspartame because you have been brainwashed to think it is harmless. (Aspartame is the principal ingredient in sugar substitutes such as NutriSweet and Equal.) Unfortunately, that is what advertising has persuaded most people to believe. How can it be that something allowed to be so widely advertised on television can be harmful? Unfortunately again, almost everything that is advertised for human consumption on television is harmful to your health in one way or another. There are very few exceptions.

Aspartame is in more than 4,000 foods today. Alarming quantities are consumed annually. Aspartame is one of the most widely consumed synthetic chemicals in the United States. Aspartame is particularly harmful in soft drinks. When dissolved, it rapidly decomposes. Within eight weeks, the aspartame in carbonated beverages has decomposed about 38 percent (about 10 percent of the by-product is methanol, which is an extremely toxic substance that can have serious side effects to the eyes and central nervous system). "So what?," you ask, the Food and Drug Administration (FDA) says it is harmless. Since aspartame has been classified as a food additive rather than a drug, no testing on human beings is required before approval for human consumption, and the adverse reactions do not have to be reported to the FDA. It makes one think there might be some politics involved.

To date, the FDA has received more than 5,000 complaints from consumers. Almost 75 percent of these complaints involved neurological and behavioral problems including headaches, dizziness, visual disturbances, mood alterations, and even some cases of seizures. Because this is such a controversial issue, the FDA refuses to hold public meetings about it or to be interviewed regarding the subject.

Most of the complaints have been received since aspartame was approved for sale in beverages such as diet soda. As mentioned earlier, complicated chemical reactions take place when aspartame is dissolved and then stored for a period of time. It decomposes and a small amount of the aspartame breaks down into methanol, a very toxic substance. Methanol is apparently the cause of many of the nervous system symptoms that I am seeing in the office on a daily basis. I think of several patients who had varied neurological symptoms which largely disappeared after the patient was given good nutritional care with the absence of aspartame. I also see frequent cases of headaches and mental confusion due to the ingestion of diet drinks.

I can almost hear you saying: "First he takes away my sugar, and now I can't even have aspartame. What's left for me to eat?" Well, there are plenty of *good* foods left. Anyway, what is more important to you, your health or your "sweet tooth?" After totally eliminating sweets for a few weeks, your body loses its tolerance for that kind of abuse. After this period, the ingestion of any significant amount of sweets will make you feel bad. Many of my patients have reported this to me.

Removing sweets from your diet will pay big dividends. Health is usually such a simple thing to attain if you are only willing to learn and to be patient. Health problems caused by abuse of your body over a period of years cannot be corrected overnight.

As I write tonight, I am in Alto, New Mexico, and Lynne is in San Antonio taking care of one of our grandchildren. I brought Kima (my American Eskimo dog) with me. She is good company when I am alone. Kima is lying by the side of my reclining deck chair as I relax and observe the black sky with its thousands of stars behind the wisps of thin clouds. Occasional flashes of lightning appear just beyond the Sierra Blanca peak and every once in awhile a shooting star will speed across the sky and disappear below the horizon. So many thoughts speed through my mind as I observe these phenomena. How could anyone view what I am seeing and not believe in a Supreme Intelligence that put it all together in an orderly fashion? All of us must believe and trust in someone or something greater than ourselves. The need to trust and be trusted is basic to our personalities.

While we are speaking of beauty and the feelings that it generates, let's dwell for a moment on another trait which makes us feel good inside when we give it and when we receive it—kindness. It is so easy to give and so much appreciated by those to whom we give it. Such feelings and expressions create a certain chemistry within the body which actually enhances the physical health of the donor. So what could be more beneficial to both parties than spreading a little kindness around?

Health is really such a simple thing as a general rule. We make it much more complicated than it should be. From childhood, it is implanted in our minds that our health is too complex for us to understand and that only doctors know how to care for our physical needs. Nothing could be farther from the truth! Doctors are only body mechanics who are trained to intervene after *something goes wrong. If we took more responsibility for* our own health, *disease wouldn't be as prevalent as it is and doctors would be like the Maytag repair man—sitting around waiting for a call.*

One of the reasons I am in Alto this weekend is that I am attending a medical meeting here. Seminars are being presented by specialists on various subjects. One lecture was on the drug treatment for rheumatoid diseases—like rheumatoid arthritis. After expressing his opinions on the benefits and the serious side effects of some twenty or thirty drugs used by doctors in the treatment of these diseases, he brought out the poignant fact that 42 percent of all hospitalizations for rheumatoid arthritis patients are because of complications of the drugs used for the treatment of the disease and not for the disease itself! Now just mull that over in your mind for a moment. Wouldn't it appear possible that some of the treatments we are using are more dangerous than the disease? Maybe that's too sensible.

The medical profession has only a little bit of knowledge about how the body works. Yet physicians are very prone to "jump on the bandwagon" and prescribe every new drug that comes down the pike (knowing that many of them may be off the market shortly due to side effects) and never stop to think that we may be doing more harm than good.

Since doctors are trained only in recognition and treatment of disease instead of in the maintenance of health, they tend to ridicule any of the simple and natural things people can do for themselves as unscientific or quackery. At least that kind of treatment doesn't put people in the hospital! But drug therapy is all most doctors know.

I have had a great many requests from my patients for a simple explanation of the purpose of each of the vitamins and how they can be used practically. I am fully aware that volumes have been written on this subject. However, in the very limited space in the chapters that follow, I will try to present a few understandable paragraphs on the most common vitamins with some description of practical uses from my own experience.

First, I want to give you a little bit of general information on vitamins. Webster's dictionary definition is "any number of unrelated, complex organic substances found variously in most foods, or sometimes synthesized in the body, and essential for the regulation of the metabolism and normal growth and function of the body." This definition was first given by C. Funk in 1913. However, it was to a certain extent a misnomer. The word vita means life and the amine comes from amino acid. It was at first thought that all vitamins contained amino acids, but that has been proven not to be true. The definition has stuck through the years, and it doesn't really make any difference as long as we understand that vitamins are essential to life and if there is a deficiency of any of the vitamins for an extended period of time, the body will begin to exhibit, first, signs of subclinical disease and later, full-blown disease.

More and more articles and "discoveries" are being made by orthodox medical research regarding the necessity of certain vitamins and minerals in the prevention and treatment of many diseases. At this time, orthodox medicine is beginning to realize the importance of vitamins and minerals to our health. They are being talked about more and more on television, in newspapers, and in medical journals. Ironically, the FDA, food and drug companies, and orthodox medicine itself is spending untold amounts of money trying to convince you, the public, that vitamins are dangerous and could be very toxic if taken in quantities larger than that recommended by the FDA. Since vitamins can't be patented, you might begin to get the idea that somebody has an axe to grind!

3

Vitamin A

Vitamin A is absolutely essential in adequate quantities for the proper and healthful functioning of the mucous membranes, skin, eyes, kidneys, gall bladder, and the immune system. Mucous membranes line all the cavities of our bodies—mouth, throat, stomach, small intestine, colon, vagina, and gall bladder. The skin is more than just a covering to keep the body from falling apart. It is an essential organ of the body with many important functions. Vitamin A is necessary in adequate quantities to prevent acne; ulcers in the mouth, stomach, or intestine; kidney stones; night blindness; eye diseases; stunted growth; and lessened resistance to disease of all kinds. It is one of the important antioxidants. (Oxidants and antioxidants are discussed in detail in Chapter 5.)

Vitamin A is a fat-soluble vitamin and therefore must use fat in the diet to properly utilize and absorb it. Vitamin A deficiencies are becoming more frequent since all this questionable ballyhoo is being publicized about extremely low-fat diets. The latest craze (and it is just that) is to eliminate all eggs, liver, butter, and the normal fats which the body has thrived on for thousands of years and replace them with man-made substitutes that are slowly killing us (but making lots of companies rich). Since vitamin A depends on the natural fats for absorption, it is only reasonable to recognize that more vitamin A deficiencies will occur in the absence of adequate fat intake. Vitamin A is found in two forms—beta carotene and vitamin A itself. Beta carotene is converted by the liver to vitamin A. If the liver is not in good health, the conversion cannot be properly done and a deficiency can result. Beta carotene is found richly in green and leafy vegetables and in orange and yellow fruits. Vitamin A is found abundantly in eggs, liver, and the fish liver oils such as cod liver oil and halibut liver oil. No conversion by the liver is necessary for the utilization of vitamin A. Many of the foods rich in vitamin A are the very foods modern medicine is telling us to eliminate. It doesn't make sense!

Over the years, I have seen many satisfying results obtained from the use of vitamin A. I have seen many teenagers whose lives had been miserable because of acne, blackheads, and other skin problems. Most of them had been treated by conventional means with creams and antibiotics to no permanent avail. These same patients have been assisted greatly with adequate doses of vitamin A, zinc, and dietary correction.

I can remember a man who was having repeated formation and passage of kidney stones every few weeks. He had undergone several surgeries to remove the stones. He had been taken off calcium, which was not the cause of the problem. Correction of his diet and adequate vitamin A, zinc, magnesium and B6 supplementation resulted in no more formation of stones. To my knowledge he has had no problems since.

About two years ago, a man who made his living as a traveling salesman came to me with a very serious eye problem. His eyes were so swollen, painful, and light sensitive that he could only keep them open a few seconds at a time, even while driving. While sitting in my office for the first time, he was constantly blinking to protect his eyes from the fluorescent lighting. He had been treated unsuccessfully with all the standard treatments, such as antibiotics, cortisone, and eye washes. After examining this patient, it was obvious that he had a vitamin A deficiency. I gave him huge doses of vitamin A and adequate zinc, and he responded very quickly. Within a few weeks, he was driving without difficulty and had no more eye pain.

Chronic sinusitis and many other conditions too numerous to recount here also respond beautifully to large doses of vitamin A along with some lifestyle changes. Suffice it to say that this vitamin is extremely important to your health.

You are probably wondering what the proper dose of vitamin A should be. That is difficult to say. Roger Williams, who wrote many great books on nutrition and taught in seminars until age ninety, discovered many years ago that the quantity of vitamins each person needs is different because of factors such as genetics, environment, previous health, and the ability to absorb and utilize food. He coined the term "biochemical individuality." Most physicians who do nutritional work think that about 20,000 to 25,000 units of vitamin A is good maintenance and that much larger doses are needed at times to correct certain conditions.

Most of you who have watched a lot of television or have read many newspapers lately are acutely aware of all the propaganda about vitamin intoxication which is being broadcast. Let me assure you that the dangers are vastly overrated and in many cases absolutely false. Anyone who has spent many years doing nutritional therapy knows that it is extremely difficult to get any vitamin intoxication at all, even with vitamins A and D. These are scare tactics by some of the big moneyed interests.

Adelle Davis, one of the foremost nutritionists of our day and author of several outstanding books on health subjects, devoted several pages in *Vitality Through Planned Nutrition* to the topic of vitamin A intoxication. She wrote, "Massive doses of vitamin A have caused no harmful effects. A group of babies fed 166,666 international units of carotene daily for five months thrived on it. Rats have been given 500,000 units of carotene daily throughout their life span, and no toxicity resulted. This amount would be equivalent to a 100 pound person taking 100,000,000 units daily. Equal amounts of vitamin A from fish liver oils have also been given to animals without harm. Such quantities of vitamin A are never given to people."

When a supposed case of vitamin A toxicity is found, it is almost always from taking huge doses of *synthetic* vitamin A over a very prolonged period. This circumstance will not happen under proper supervision. Even though chemists say there is no difference between synthetic vitamin A and the natural vitamin A found in fish liver oils, the body definitely knows the difference and utilizes the fish liver oils without problems.

My wife, Lynne, tells me that I do too much "preaching" when I write. Maybe I do, but in my own defense, let me tell you a little story. In 1939, just before I graduated from Hollywood High School in California, I was quite uncertain about what my calling in life should be. So I took an aptitude test which was offered to the students who were about to graduate. Guess what—according to the test results, the vocation for which I had the most aptitude was preaching. Second was social work and third was medicine. As fate would have it I became a doctor, but I guess I at least have a legitimate excuse to do a little preaching.

A few weeks ago, Lynne and I were sitting in the church we attend when we are in Ruidoso, N.M. The theme of the sermon was the constant vigilance it takes in our personal lives to develop qualities that would make us acceptable citizens of heaven. I was thinking about this after the service and the thought came to mind that there is a very pertinent parallel to our health. Health, in most cases, is not something that we just happen to have. Similarly, disease is not something that we just happen to get. Health is something that we can influence by personal responsibility. We must strive for it. We should be continually aware that our thinking habits, our eating habits, and our exercise habits have a direct, although at times delayed, effect on the way our bodies operate. It is certainly true that some people are more blessed with good genetics than others, but that is no logical excuse to neglect the positive things that we can do to become relatively pain and disease free.

So many times I have heard people say that they had never had any serious health problems until they became thirty or forty years old, and then, everything just started "falling apart at the seams." What they didn't realize is that they had been mistreating their bodies for those thirty or forty years and finally their physical and chemical reserves were depleted to the point the body could no longer derive adequate nourishment from an already bankrupt reserve system. The human body is a marvelous piece of machinery. But when its limits are exceeded, disease is waiting to manifest itself.

Ever since its inception, the medical profession has been looking for the answers to sickness with a mistaken and misguided philosophy. Bacteria and viruses are not the basic cause of disease, and neither are medications the way to good health. A weakened immune system is the basic cause of most ill health. If our immune system protection was in perfect condition, we would never get sick. But of course, those ideal conditions can never exist. It is true that bacteria and viruses are present when disease strikes, but they are not the real cause of the problem. They are only opportunists that take advantage of a weakened immune system. If they were the underlying cause of disease, everyone who harbors that specific bacteria would be ill with that particular disease. This is definitely not the case. Ten people can be exposed to a particular infection and maybe only four or five people contract it. Why? This misguided philosophy is not likely to change since it is much more profitable to treat sick people than it is to keep people well. So much for preaching.

4

The B Complex Vitamins

A precise definition of *vitamin B* is quite difficult because it is of necessity vague. The word *vitamin* merely means an organic substance necessary for the maintenance of life. However, the B vitamins are several in number. They have some effects in common and a deficiency of any one of them can cause specific symptoms and "diseases." Hence, a reasonable definition for vitamin B is: "A water-soluble substance found abundantly in liver, whole grains, and brewer's yeast, which aids in the utilization of proteins, carbohydrates, and fats."

The best source of vitamin B, as with other vitamins, is whole, unprocessed foods. Generally speaking, good sources of vitamin B are liver, whole grains, beans, legumes, nuts, brewer's yeast, and eggs. This is why I constantly emphasize the importance of staying out of the middle aisles of the grocery store when you do your shopping. Most of the good foods are found on the perimeter aisles. You will also note that many of the above listed foods are considered "forbidden fruit" by the medical profession which is now on a profitable, but in my opinion, very foolish anti-cholesterol campaign. (See Chapter 9).

When most people think of vitamin B, energy and nerves generally come to mind. This is right, because vitamin B is certainly important in these two areas. However, vitamin B complex deficiencies can cause lots of problems in other areas also. Some of these problems include fatigue, depression, constipation, nervousness, mental confusion, skin problems, hair loss, birth defects, convulsive seizures, loss of appetite, sore tongue and mouth, burning feet, toxemia of pregnancy, liver problems, and some other less recognized symptoms.

Thiamin (B1) is particularly important in helping prevent or overcome fatigue, loss of appetite, burning extremities, and nervous system degeneration. Thiamin is found richly in brewer's yeast, liver, whole grains, and peanuts.

Riboflavin (B2) is particularly important in helping prevent some skin problems such as cracks in the corners of the mouth and scaling around the eyebrows and nose. Dandruff is also a common complaint of this deficiency. Found richly in organ meats, almonds, broccoli, and the other foods mentioned above. Vitamin B2 turns the urine a very bright yellow color which is nothing to be concerned about.

Niacin and Niacinamide are particularly important in treating depression, certain skin problems, mental confusion, and fatigue. They are found in all those foods mentioned for B1. Most of the functions of the two are the same except for two very noticeable differences.

1. Large doses of Niacin, particularly when taken on an empty stomach, can cause a "niacin flush." Niacin flush is a reddening of the skin accompanied by a burning sensation and sometimes itching, caused by a dilation of the blood vessels in the skin. It is harmless and disappears in about 45 minutes or less but can be frightening to a patient who does not understand what is happening.

2. Niacinamide does *not* have a cholesterol-lowering effect. Niacin does.

Pyridoxine (B6) is an extremely important vitamin in the treatment of fluid retention, cystic and painful breasts, certain cases of epileptic seizures, depression, learning disabilities (such as hyperactivity or Attention Deficit Disorder), autism, and hypoglycemia. B6 is an especially important vitamin. It is found richly in most of the "forbidden" foods mentioned above plus pecans, peanuts, bananas, and beans.

Cyanocobalamin (B12) is very important in the treatment of fatigue, loss of appetite, sore tongue, irritability, mental confusion, senility symptoms, and some anemias. The B vitamins —particularly B12—are important in older people whose digestive systems are incapable of absorbing the nutrition from even the good foods. Many times injections of these vitamins have a profound and dramatic effect. The B vitamins are found richly in eggs, fish, and liver—again, the "forbidden" foods. It is amazing to me that all of these health-giving vitamins are found so abundantly in so many of the foods orthodox medicine has put on the forbidden list. *Something must be wrong* with either God or the medical profession. I wonder which?

Folic acid (no number has been given to this vitamin) is very important for preventing birth defects, anemia, fatigue, and digestive problems. Folic acid is found abundantly in green and leafy vegetables, liver, eggs, and whole grains. This vitamin is just now beginning to be recognized by the medical profession because of its importance in preventing birth defects. And, it is now a common topic for articles in women's magazines and for television reports. As usual, this information is being distributed about forty or fifty years too late.

Pantothenic acid (B5) is another vitamin that is now beginning to assume some importance. It is extremely valuable for strengthening the immune system, and is useful for treating allergies and inflammatory diseases such as rheumatoid arthritis. It is found in all of the "forbidden" foods plus whole grains.

I feel it is unwise to try to give the proper doses of these vitamins without being acquainted with the patient and the particular problem for which it is being used. However, with the exception of vitamins A and D, the ideal intake is probably at least ten times the RDA and in certain conditions, much more than that.

The B vitamins are very safe. The occasional case of so-called "toxicity" that is blown out of proportion on television by the media doctors is generally because of ignorance on their part. They get paid to say what the orthodoxy wants them to say. The rare case of toxicity that might be valid is always due to someone taking inordinate amounts of a single vitamin for a very long period of time without balancing the dose with the other necessary vitamins and without any supervision from a nutritionally oriented physician. These cases are never lethal anyway. Compare that to the *thousands* of *deaths* each year from prescription drugs that get no publicity at all. I guess it depends on whose ox is getting gored.

MEMORIAL TO DR. LINUS PAULING

You may not realize it, but you and I lost a good friend. Dr. Linus Pauling died in the summer of 1994 at the age of ninety-three. Many of you, no, I would say most of you, probably have no idea how much you are in his debt. Dr. Pauling was a brilliant biochemist and the only person ever to have the distinction of winning two unshared Nobel Prizes. The first in 1954 for his research into the nature of chemical bonds. The second in 1962 for his fight against nuclear testing and against warfare as a means of settling international disputes. He made many great scientific discoveries for which he was applauded by the international scientific community. However, the research he did from which you personally have benefited the most is his work on what he termed "orthomolecular medicine"—the theory that larger than normal amounts of particular micronutrients and other substances present in the body could be used in the successful treatment and prevention of certain diseases including heart disease and cancer.

The most famous nutrient on which he spent so much of his research since the 1960s is vitamin C. Now you may be beginning to get a clue as to why you owe him so much. In 1970, he wrote the very controversial book "Vitamin C and the Common Cold" which was an instant best seller. Ironically, though the truth made manifest in this book has helped millions of people to escape many different illnesses, its truths were never accepted by the people who need it the most—the medical profession. Dr. Pauling was a fighter for truth and was never deterred from his mission just because he met ridicule and disbelief from the very profession he was trying to teach. But the truth will eventually conquer long after the disbelievers and mockers have been proven wrong.

The New England Journal of Medicine, one of the most ardent critics of Dr. Pauling's work on vitamin C, has finally been obliged to "eat their words." In a recent edition, even they suggest that vitamins C, A, E and beta carotene may reduce the incidence of heart trouble and cancer. However, even to this day, no credit is given to Dr. Pauling for the research upon which this conclusion is based. It is sad how much egotism and stubbornness characterize the medical profession.

Dr. Pauling died of cancer. There are probably those who will still scoff at his teachings because much of his work was directed to show how vitamin C could prevent or delay cancer. They will say, "See, the old man died of cancer." Dr. Pauling had been taking between 18,000 and 20,000 mg. of vitamin C ever since I first met him about twenty years ago. All of us have to die sometime from something. When Dr. Pauling found out he had prostate cancer several years ago, he made the comment that there was no way of knowing how much his life had been prolonged because he had taken large amounts of vitamin C daily since his research started many years ago. Let me remind you that up until the last year of his life he was still very active in research and study that would benefit mankind.

He lived what he preached, and it certainly showed. How many of his scoffers can match his achievements? Much of what I have learned about nutritional therapy, and especially about the use of vitamin C in the treatment and prevention of so many diseases, was learned from Dr. Pauling. Many of you owe a debt of gratitude to this outstanding old gentleman for what he has taught you through me. It is not only you who owe him a debt of gratitude. I do also. I have no doubt that many of the things that I have learned from him have kept me alive to see my seventy-fourth birthday pass with a vigorous and active lifestyle.

As I sit here on the deck of my mountain home, watching the half moon gradually disappear behind the silhouette of the distant Sacramento Mountain Range, I can't help but think about how much all of our lives are influenced by those we touch—many of whom we have never had the chance to thank. This is certainly true of Dr. Pauling. Millions of people all over the world, and certainly my patients, have been benefited by the work that he did. It is too bad that you couldn't have thanked him yourself. He would have appreciated that.

So, we lift our hearts in tribute and thanks to that grand gentleman, Dr. Linus Carl Pauling.

5

Vitamin C

Your very life is dependent on adequate dietary intake of vitamin C. The biochemical actions of vitamin C are varied and complicated. So much so in fact, that brilliant biochemists like Linus Pauling, Ph.D., have spent a good part of their scientific lives investigating its actions. I am certainly no biochemist, but I have spent a lot of time studying the works of these learned people and applying their findings to the practical use of helping my patients, and myself, to more optimal health.

First, I'll briefly explain how vitamin C works. Both oxidants and antioxidants are found in the human body. Oxidants in our bodies cause chemical reactions that damage or destroy living cells. The purpose of antioxidants is to prevent our cells from being damaged by the oxidants.

Oxidants and antioxidants can come from normal physiologic processes within the body or from external sources. Examples of oxidants from external sources are toxic chemicals we breathe (such as cigarette smoke and exhaust fumes) and toxins in our food and water. Among the principle sources of external antioxidants are vitamin C, vitamin E, beta carotene, vitamin A and selenium. Of course, there are many others but these are some of the most important ones.

Within our bodies, a constant battle goes on between oxidants and antioxidants. That is why *antioxidants are so vital to our health and longevity*! According to the Linus Pauling Institute of Science and Medicine, vitamin C has been found to be the *only* antioxidant in our blood plasma that completely protects us from the ravages of oxidants. In addition to its importance as an antioxidant, vitamin C is essential to the body's formation of connective tissue and to the maintenance of a strong immune system, which protects our bodies from disease and infection.

The amount of health and protection from disease that one derives from the intake of vitamin C depends to a large extent on the quantity taken. If a body is under severe attack from oxidants due to bad living habits, stress, smoking, etc., it may take several thousand milligrams (mg.) of vitamin C a day to furnish enough antioxidant action to destroy the oxidants. If, on the other hand, we have better eating and living habits and fewer oxidants to destroy, less vitamin C is needed. For instance, it is estimated that about 40 mg. of vitamin C is needed to counteract the oxidant effect of *one* cigarette. A person who smokes two packs a day will need about 1,600 mg. of vitamin C just to try to take care of the cigarettes, and that doesn't leave any for the necessities of the body.

Vitamin C is manufactured within the body of almost every animal *except* the human being. We do not have the capability to make vitamin C, so we are absolutely dependent upon foods and supplementation to furnish our bodies with an adequate amount to give us optimal health. These amounts vary depending on the biochemical individuality of each person and the lifestyle of that person.

In yesteryear, before vitamin C was discovered and isolated, the sailors on ships crossing the ocean died from scurvy after being on board ship for months at a time without access to fresh foods. Later, it was discovered that if they included a few limes (which contain vitamin C) in their diet on board ship, they didn't get sick. This is how the Englishman got the name "limey." While it is true that full blown scurvy is rarely seen in this country anymore, I see on a daily basis evidence of subclinical scurvy. These are patients who have enough vitamin C intake to prevent outright scurvy but not enough to prevent the bleeding gums, loose teeth, easy bruising, aching and inflamed joints, and fatigue associated with lower than adequate intake of this vitamin.

Vitamin C is good for so many conditions that it would be difficult to list them all. First, it is absolutely essential to life, so it therefore follows that although life can be maintained on minimal amounts, optimal health cannot. Linus Pauling's Institute has conclusively proven that less than adequate amounts of vitamin C cause the connective tissue structure in the arteries to weaken, which results in a break down of the artery's lining. Subsequently, cholesterol sticks to the artery walls and plaques gradually build up. These events ultimately result in a heart attack. The interesting thing that has been demonstrated is that the weakened artery—due to inadequate vitamin C—was the basic cause of the cholesterol build up and the resultant heart attack, not the cholesterol itself.

Vitamin C is very essential to a strong immune system, and I use a lot of it both intravenously and orally for my patients. This vitamin is utilized with calcium and magnesium to build healthy connective tissue and joints. Therefore, vitamin C is useful in the prevention and treatment of arthritis. I see many cases of spontaneous bruising, which is alleviated with proper vitamin C therapy.

Vitamin C deficiency is probably the most frequently seen deficiency in my office because so few people eat enough *raw* fruits and vegetables. It is important to remember that vitamin C is largely destroyed in cooking and storage.

Now is where the controversy comes in. Orthodox medicine has always claimed that because only a minute amount of vitamin C is necessary to prevent scurvy, no more is necessary for health. Their theory apparently is that if you don't have scurvy and you are alive, you are healthy. This kind of thinking is absurd! There are all shades of gray between death from lack of vitamin C and optimal health with an adequate amount.

There is now so much proof that larger than minimal doses of vitamin C are protective to our health—and even curative in many cases—that even orthodox medicine is beginning to recognize it. More articles are now being published in medical journals that tout the power of vitamin C in helping to prevent arthritis, cancer, and many other degenerative conditions.

The amount of vitamin C necessary to do its part in providing optimal health is still a very controversial subject. During his lifetime, Dr. Linus Pauling probably did more scientific research on vitamin C than any other person. He always contended that everyone should take at least 2,000 to 3,000 mg. daily for good health. For the last twenty to twenty-five years of his life, he made it a daily practice to take about 20,000 mg. of vitamin C. He was active and vibrant until shortly before he died in 1994. Not everyone can take that large a dose without having diarrhea, but Dr. Pauling was never concerned about toxicity from large doses of vitamin C, even though the Recommended Daily Allowance (RDA) is only about 40 mg. I take between 3,000 and 5,000 mg. daily in addition to eating large amounts of fresh fruits and vegetables, and I am not doing too badly at age seventy-four.

Dr. Pauling recommended that at the first sign of a cold or infection, vitamin C intake should be increased to 500 to 1,000 mg. per hour, which translates into about 10,000 to 15,000 mg. per day. High tissue levels, which enhance our immunity to infection, are thus maintained even though some of the excess vitamin C is eliminated from the body in the urine and perspiration.

My clinical experience with the use of vitamin C both orally and intravenously, has been very extensive and quite productive in assisting the restoration and maintenance of health for thousands of my patients over the years. Vitamin C should not be taken only when an illness if present. It will do very little good that way. High tissue levels of vitamin C must be maintained if it is to have protective powers. If adequate tissue levels are maintained constantly, it is then helpful to take additional vitamin C under conditions of excess stress, toxicity, or illness. I cannot overemphasize the importance of *daily* intake of vitamin C in adequate amounts.

I wouldn't want you to get the idea that I think vitamin C is the answer to all illness, because I don't. However, I certainly do believe that your general health is dependent to a large extent on adequate intake of this very valuable chemical. So many things enter into the equation of attaining and maintaining good health.

Again I am reveling in the almost phantasmic beauty that so inspires my thinking. As I sit on the deck in the late of the evening, the moon has not yet come up and the complete absence of any light in this high mountain area imparts a complete blackness to the sky which is punctuated by what appears to be thousands of stars. My thoughts begin to ramble but finally focus. All of us need occasional periods of solitude when we can just relax and appreciate the order and discipline which God has built into the workings of the universe and His creations. Without the recognition of the abundance with which we have been blessed, it becomes difficult to separate the really important things in our lives from the seemingly important (but really inconsequential) things. We have a human tendency to take, so much of the time, and appreciate so little of the time.

No matter how self-sufficient we may think we are, there are so many people that we all depend on for so many things and yet it is probably a rare circumstance when we tell them so. It seems so easy to criticize but so difficult to praise. How often do we express our love in meaningful ways to our husbands, wives, children, brothers, and sisters? Yet, these are some of the most important people in our lives and probably the only people who will really miss us very long after we are gone.

On a compact disc by Perry Como called "Perry Como Today" is a song called "The Wind Beneath My Wings" and the words express so much the way I feel about my wife and children. I won't quote it all, but it ends like this: "Did you ever know that you're my hero, and everything I'd like to be. I can fly higher than an eagle, because you are the wind beneath my wings." All of us need motivation to endure many of the difficult situations that arise and what better motivation could we have? Everybody depends on somebody.

Although these philosophical sessions don't give you information on tangible things that you can "hang your hat on," I feel they are important because our thinking and our mental attitude is so important to our physical well-being.

Whatever career and success I have had in the medical field in my forty-three years of practice—the first five in Sundown, Texas and the balance in Lubbock, Texas—I owe to the thousands of people who have entrusted me with their lives and their health. Hopefully, most of these people are also my friends. I truly appreciate them and their trust and hope that our relationship has resulted in a better quality of life for all of us.

While I am on the subject of appreciation, I must add one very personal note. Lynne and I have been married fifty-two years and have been blessed with five wonderful children, eleven grandchildren, and two great grandchildren with another "in the hanger." They have been the center of our lives and still are. Besides being a wonderful and enduring wife, Lynne has been the most wonderful mother a child could ever hope for. I think all of our children would say amen to that.

6

Vitamin E: The Long-Ridiculed Lifesaver

It's interesting, but in a way unfortunate, how so many things that are necessary and even lifesaving to patients are at first ridiculed by orthodox medicine and then, after many years, "discovered" by that same group and pronounced to be a new breakthrough in overcoming the diseases that afflict mankind. So it is with vitamin E.

I can remember more than fifty years ago when my father, who was an osteopathic physician and did a lot of nutritional work, used vitamin E for many of his patients and got excellent results. Then, for the next thirty-five years, orthodox medicine ridiculed its use and anyone who used it. Vitamin E was not even considered necessary for human nutrition. About fifteen years ago, the powers that be admitted that vitamin E was an essential nutrient but that 15 mg. a day was all that was needed for good nutrition.

Those of us who took and used hundreds of milligrams a day were still on the fringes of respectability. Only lately has the "new discovery" been made by *their* research that vitamin E in large doses is actually therapeutic for many conditions. Things have finally come full circle and we "quacks" are now vindicated. The tragic thing about it is that while orthodoxy had its collective head in the sand, millions of people with heart trouble, vascular problems, eye problems, muscular problems, immune disorders, and other ailments have suffered because they were deprived of its benefits.

Vitamin E is a potent antioxidant, second only to vitamin C. Extensive research work with vitamin E has been done by the Shute brothers (doctors in Canada). They documented more than 25,000 cases of heart trouble treated beneficially with vitamin E. They also did research with burn victims where vitamin E was used to prevent or greatly lessen scarring and speed healing.

The uses of vitamin E are so numerous that it would be impossible in such a short chapter to document them all. The doses necessary to obtain results also vary greatly. Vitamin E is nontoxic in its natural form. This vitamin is sold as dl-alpha tocopheryl, d-alpha tocopherol, and mixed tocopherols (vitamin E complex). The complex contains all four fractions of vitamin E—alpha, beta, gamma, and delta. The latter three fractions contain most of the antioxidant effect. The synthetic form (dl) is probably the most poorly utilized. I use only the "complex." Vitamin E is extremely safe. I have never seen a case of toxicity from it no matter what the dose. I have taken 800 units a day of the complex for years.

Disease conditions become diseases not just from the lack of one or two nutrients. Generally, there are a multitude of factors involved that have to be changed in order to bring a patient back to health. So, having said that, I will enumerate some of the things for which I find vitamin E very useful in the treatment of my patients.

- **Leg cramps**. Along with magnesium and calcium, vitamin E is extremely effective because it increases the circulation in the small blood vessels.

- **Cystic breasts**. Over a period of time, vitamin E, along with other nutritional measures, helps to decrease the size of the cysts or eliminate them altogether.

- **Burns**. I have seen vitamin E completely prevent scarring from bad burns when used both topically and internally. It also softens and reduces scarring which has already formed.

- **Muscular and connective tissue problems**. Many of these problems, such as fibromyositis and fibromyalgia rheumatica, require large doses but respond gradually, especially when other nutrients and lifestyle changes are made.

- **Phlebitis**. I have personally treated several severe cases of phlebitis both in hospitalized patients and outpatients with what would be considered extremely large doses of vitamin E with almost complete clearing of the vascular hardening and tenderness in as little as a week.

- **Repeated spontaneous abortion (miscarriage)**. Miscarriage is frequently caused by low levels of vitamin E in the body. I remember a lady who had five miscarriages without a successful pregnancy until she took vitamin E for several months before her next conception, which resulted in a healthy, full-term pregnancy.

Contrary to public belief and numerous jokes, vitamin E is *not* an aphrodisiac in the commonly accepted meaning of the word. It is, however, essential for the health of the reproductive system.

Vitamin E is essential to the efficient functioning of the heart and hence is indispensable to life. It protects us against the bad effects of too many polyunsaturated fats. We have been brainwashed to believe that only unsaturated fats are protective to our hearts. This is not true. Some unsaturated fat is helpful, but some saturated fat is necessary also and not the villain the food companies would have us believe. This is just another of the money making propaganda that is being fed to a puzzled public.

Pure virgin olive oil is the best oil to use in cooking and or in salad dressings. Olive oil is not a polyunsaturated fat. Although the polyunsaturated fats have been pushed onto the public for many years as a preventive for heart trouble, heart trouble is as prevalent as ever—probably more so. That ought to tell us something; but we don't learn easily, especially when profit propaganda is involved. Just remember that adequate vitamin E protects us against the harmful effects of too much polyunsaturated fat. A certain amount of natural polyunsaturated fat is necessary for our health, but the heat refining methods used on the oils found in the grocery store change the character of the fats. Research has shown that they then become capable of causing atherosclerosis in our blood vessels, which is the very thing they are advertised to prevent. I suggest that people use only cold pressed oils for cooking purposes and take adequate vitamin E.

One of my patients asked me why there is so much heart failure today. The answer is very complex. Maybe there is more being diagnosed in recent years and maybe we are just seeing it publicized more for many reasons. The ultimate answer to most heart problems can probably be found in genetics and lifestyle (which includes nutrition). While genetics are very important, even some of the bad genetics can be altered with good living habits. We poison our bodies from every side these days. Besides the extremely dangerous habits of smoking and sitting on our backside when we should be getting exercise, we are drinking water that is chemically treated, we are breathing air that is polluted with all kinds of chemicals, we eat foods that are highly refined and from which many of the nutrients have been removed, we drink inordinate amounts of soft drinks, we sugar and aspartame our bodies to death, and then on top of all that we ingest huge amounts of medicines which many times do more harm than good. Until we get wise and start to take responsibility for our own health, we will be a sick and overfed nation. And all the government "wisdom" in the world will not help us!

JUNE 11 7:30 P.M. *Hello. As I write, Lynne and I are 35,000 feet in the air over the Atlantic Ocean on the way to Switzerland to celebrate our 50th wedding anniversary! I don't take many extended vacations—usually only two or three days at a time. I feel a little guilty and uneasy about leaving things at home unattended for ten days. I have thought in the back of my mind that there may be some of my patients who need me and that I should be there to help—I'm probably feeling more egotism than reality.*

We have been flying for many hours and the sun is beginning its descent below the horizon. The vast ocean below appears like a solid mass of smooth blue with only a very occasional whitecap discernible. Through the headset, the soft strains of "Home On The Range" is playing. I don't recall ever really thinking about the words before, particularly the first part of the song: "How often at night with the heavens so bright by the light from the glittering stars, have I sat there amazed and asked as I gazed, if their glory exceeds that of ours." What unbelievable and enigmatic wonders the universe holds for us to try to fathom and enjoy. How ironic and sad that just a few hundred miles from where we will be experiencing the serenity and beauty of a friendly little village in the heart of the Alps, the Bosnians and the Serbs will be maiming and killing each other. If only we could share with them some of the joy and love that we feel. I guess it's not to be.

As I sit here next to the woman I have loved for more than 50 years, cruising over the Atlantic Ocean at about 600 miles per hour, I am wondering, where all the years have gone? How could we possibly have grandchildren who are married and starting to raise their own families? The years have gone by so fast, and so many of life's memorable moments seem as if they happened only yesterday.

When I was forty, I looked at people my age and thought how old that is! However, as I view it from this end of the spectrum, I see it quite differently. My mind still tells me that I am young, but in certain areas I know that my body doesn't respond as readily as it once did. I suppose I notice it mostly in the sports I enjoy. My mind tells me what I should do, but my body seems to have lost some of its agility. I'm sure some of my older patients can relate to that. But, just because we are aging chronologically, doesn't mean that our bodies should have to "play out on us." I would love to see all of my patients, both young and old, feel as good as I do. We always dream much more than we can accomplish, but at least I can continue to dream and some of it will come true.

Well, we have been traveling East all this very short night. The captain has just flashed some interesting statistics on the movie screen. It is now 7:30 a.m. at our present location over the Atlantic. The time at home is 1:30 a.m. (when we should be sleeping soundly in our beds). Ground speed is 597 miles per hour and the temperature outside the airplane is minus 67 degrees Fahrenheit (67 below zero). I'm glad we're inside!

I think the thin air must be getting to me. I am thinking, here I am with a lot more years behind me than in front of me. How should success in this life be measured? By money? I think not, because money has no lasting value of itself. By the power one attains or the position he or she holds in life? I don't think so, because the grave makes no differentiation between the weak or the powerful. I think that our true value will be measured by an entirely different yardstick.

Did we give of ourselves to someone because we loved them?

Have we tried to instill in our children the capacity to love and be generous with themselves and what possessions they may have acquired?

Have we demonstrated the ability to forgive and felt the joy of doing so?

Have we been kind to other people as much as is reasonably possible?

Have we given of our skills and talents to help others who are less fortunate?

Have we demonstrated an appreciation for the many things that are done for us?

Have we been able to recognize the human fault within ourselves and not blame others for our misfortunes?

Have we been an example for good to most of those with whom we have come in contact?

Have we earned the reputation of being honest and dependable?

Have we gained the respect and love of our children?

Have we been true to ourselves no matter what the consequences?

Have we lived in such a way that most of those who know us will be truly sorry when we are gone?

If we can answer yes to most of these questions, then life has indeed been a success.

JUNE 13 10:30 P.M. *If I couldn't see a few electric lights and a few modern amenities as I sit on the deck of my hotel room in Kandersteg, Switzerland, a quaint Swiss village, I wouldn't know I was in the 20th century. This little village, immediately surrounded on all sides by gigantic, rugged, 15,000 ft. snow-capped peaks, makes all my efforts to describe it very futile. Amid all this beauty and serenity, it is difficult to understand how we can so little appreciate what God has given us to enjoy.*

If we could pause for just a few moments each day to look beyond ourselves, many of our stress-related problems would vanish with no need for doctors or medications. If I could just convey that peace to all of you, so many problems would disappear. I wish it for all of you.

JUNE 18. *As we travel around Switzerland, it becomes quite evident that people are people the world over. All have personal desires, and all are trying to fulfill their wants and* *needs by utilizing the talents they have. In the small mountain villages, we notice a very refreshing environment. There seems to be no crime or fear of having your belongings stolen. Merchants display their merchandise on the sidewalks outside their shops unattended, with no apparent worry of anyone taking anything without bringing it into the shop to pay for it. Some businesses even leave things out overnight! What a good feeling to know that there is still trust in this world. Of course, we are jolted back to life when we go to the big cities and find the same discouraging problems of drugs and crime that we have in our country, but probably not to the same extent.*

Even though we are thousands of miles from the USA and many other things may change, the wonders of nature stay the same for all people to enjoy. I see the same big shining Venus hanging over the beautiful Alps peak that I see while sitting on my deck in Alto, New Mexico, looking at its beauty over the peak of Sierra Blanca. I haven't lost my love for my "little bit of heaven."

JUNE 19. *We have just taken the chair lift to one of the high mountain peaks above the little village of Kandersteg. As I survey these natural wonders with their exhilarating beauty, I feel like I am at the side of God observing all that He has created. Words cannot describe what I am feeling at this moment. How does one count one's blessings? I count mine by the multitude. Just being alive with a wonderful wife and an equally valued family is ample reward. Still having good health and the ability to be useful in helping people is an added blessing.*

JUNE 20. *Although we have either been flying or waiting in airports for the past 25 hours without sleep (and we are both very tired), I can say that there are no friendlier and nicer people in this whole world than those right here in Texas. We are glad to be home.*

7

Magnesium: The 5-Cent Miracle Tablet

While a lot of information has been made available on vitamins, relatively little is ever heard about minerals. However, minerals are equally important for your health and just as useful in treating disease conditions. Probably most of you think of magnesium as a metal that is hard and used in making steel and automobiles. Magnesium is also one of the most vital substances that our bodies need for health and freedom from disease.

Magnesium is a known activator of at least 300 enzymes governing all aspects of health, including the function of cells that control the electrical activity of the heart. It is now known that most heart attack victims are low in cellular magnesium and that with the addition of magnesium to cardiac care, many lives can be saved. The balance between calcium and magnesium is extremely important. Calcium supplementation without additional magnesium can be very ineffective and even inadvisable since it requires magnesium to utilize calcium.

The purposes for which the body utilizes magnesium are so numerous that it would be impossible to list them all. I am sure we do not even know all of them. I will however, enumerate the ones that readily come to mind.

Enzyme activity. Enzymes are protein substances produced within the living organisms that serve as catalysts for cellular metabolism. The human body produces thousands of different enzymes. Hundreds of these enzymes depend upon magnesium for proper functioning.

Calcium metabolism. Calcium and magnesium in proper proportion are absolutely dependent on each other. Most everyone is aware of the necessity for adequate calcium intake. However, most people and a lot of doctors do not realize the important role that magnesium plays in the utilization of calcium. Most people get far too much calcium in relation to their magnesium intake. Excessive calcium causes the kidneys to excrete magnesium and that increases the magnesium deficiency. That is one reason I hate to see people depending on antacid tablets which contain calcium for their bodily calcium requirements. They are only further depleting their magnesium reserves. They are doing more harm than good. The more calcium you consume without adequate amounts of magnesium, the more you magnify the symptoms of magnesium deficiency. The proper ratio of calcium to magnesium intake is about two to one.

Heart rhythm irregularities. Magnesium is important in the prevention and correction of certain heart rhythm irregularities, especially tachycardia (rapid heartbeat). In some respects, magnesium accomplishes the same benefits as calcium channel blocking drugs. They help the cardiac muscle properly utilize calcium. Magnesium has two major benefits: no side effects and about 1/30th the cost.

Nerve sedation. Magnesium is one of the principal components of a healthy nervous system. "Jangled nerves" are rarely present with an adequate amount of magnesium. Insomnia can many times be overcome with 300 or 400 mg. of magnesium taken just before retiring.

Mental illness. Even moderate deficiencies in magnesium can cause nervousness, irritability, and hostility. People who are generally friendly and agreeable can become aggressive and withdrawn due to magnesium deficiency. There may be no other single deficiency which is so responsible for the widespread use of tranquilizers.

Fatigue (including Chronic Fatigue Syndrome). Magnesium is essential in the satisfactory treatment of the muscular symptoms and mental lethargy associated with this condition. Sometimes as much as 1,000 to 3,000 mg. in an intravenous infusion is used. Magnesium by mouth is also used, but large doses of magnesium taken orally can cause diarrhea.

Muscle Relaxation. Since magnesium is a muscle relaxant, it is very essential to stopping muscle cramps in the legs and back. Frequently, people take a lot of calcium or drink large quantities of milk to try to alleviate this problem. Many times, this approach only aggravates the symptoms because the excessive calcium causes a further depletion of magnesium. Just a few magnesium tablets a day is all that is needed.

High Blood Pressure. Since spasm and extra tension in the muscular walls of the vascular system is largely responsible for high blood pressure, it is beneficial to take a few hundred milligrams of magnesium daily to help relax the blood vessel walls. It may not be the only thing that is necessary, but it is certainly a useful tool in therapy.

Lowering Cholesterol Blood Levels. Lecithin allows the body to properly metabolize fats and cholesterol. However, the manufacture of lecithin requires certain enzymes which are activated by B6 and magnesium. Hence, magnesium is indirectly responsible for, but essential to, the proper metabolism of fat and integrity of the healthy blood vessel. Many times, just giving a heart patient 500 or 600 mg. of magnesium a day can produce a dramatic improvement.

Menstrual cramping and PMS problems. It is only reasonable that if magnesium can relax muscles, it can also relax the muscular wall of the uterus. Such is definitely the case. Since B6 and magnesium work together in a cooperative effort, supplementation with these essential elements can help overcome a lot of cyclical misery.

Diabetes Mellitus. Indirectly, magnesium deficiency could be a part of the cause of diabetes. Magnesium levels are particularly low in diabetics. B6 is also very essential to help prevent and cure diabetes. When B6 is not present in sufficient amounts to properly utilize tryptophane (an essential amino acid), another substance known as xanthurenic acid is formed, which is very damaging to the pancreas. It is the pancreas which produces insulin to control the blood sugar. Magnesium helps B6 to work. Also, if there is enough magnesium present, it takes much less B6 to perform its necessary function. Hence magnesium and B6 play an important role in diabetes.

Epilepsy. This is a condition in which magnesium can play a dramatic role. I have personally seen many cases of idiopathic epilepsy stopped by giving adequate doses of magnesium and vitamin B6. This vitamin and mineral combination has such a valuable synergistic effect that I rarely use one without the other. I have seen epileptic seizures of many years' duration, which had previously been treated with various anticonvulsant drugs, stop within a very short period of time after adequate supplementation of magnesium and B6. The power of nature is very great if given the proper natural ingredients with which to work.

Toxemia of pregnancy. Here again, the combination of magnesium and vitamin B6 is invaluable. Blood urea is particularly high in cases of toxemia of pregnancy. Adequate intake of magnesium and B6 is instrumental in rapidly lowering the urea level and controlling the uremic poisoning which threatens the pregnancy. During the thirty years that I practiced obstetrics, I delivered about 2,000 babies. Very few of my patients experienced problems with toxemia of pregnancy because of the protective effect of magnesium and B6.

Please keep in mind that magnesium is not the only treatment for the above conditions, but it is very useful and sometimes rapidly effective.

Inadequate time and space do not permit expounding further on the values of magnesium as proven in my clinical experience. Magnesium is depleted by the ingestion of what I term "junk foods." Practical wisdom should therefore admonish you to stay away from the foods which contain large amounts of sugar, white (enriched) flour, soft drinks (regular or diet—it makes no difference), and the numerous injurious foods which we ingest strictly for taste appeal and not nutritional value. We are constantly bombarded by television ads designed to make a profit without regard to what they are doing to our health. One of my pet admonitions to my patients is: "If it is advertised on T.V., don't eat it." This is true with very few exceptions.

While in Switzerland, I saw some of the most beautiful country the world has to offer. However, some of the rest of that beautiful country is right close to home and I am looking at it right now. The moon is completely full and some dark and white clouds are hanging over the Sierra Blanca peak. A light breeze is stirring and the temperature is a refreshing 68 degrees, and I am sitting here thinking how great it is to be alive.

I find it very easy to think these thoughts when I am surrounded by such beauty. Beautiful thoughts are inspired by a peaceful and pleasant atmosphere. It makes me very sad to know that there are millions of people all over the world who live their entire lives in crowded cities, never seeing a mountain or the beautiful pine trees, or the star-studded sky so clear in the darkness of the lightless countryside—never experiencing the awe, peace of mind, and spirit that comes with losing oneself in the ecstasy of nature.

When times are stressful and things are not going right or when some of my patients are in trouble or distress, I seek refuge in the knowledge that beauty still remains and that the God who made all of these awe-inspiring creations is still alive and well. It is we who are foolish because we don't take time to appreciate them.

When I was younger, I used to have illusions of accomplishing things that would help change the world. Lynne has always wisely reigned me in with the admonition that there is only a certain amount I can accomplish in a lifetime. Her wisdom dictates that to make this world a little better place can best be done by being patient and helping one person at a time and letting that help "trickle down" to other people who will in turn pass it on to others. And so it has been. It gives me a considerable amount of satisfaction to feel that I have been instrumental in teaching a lot of people how to overcome some of their perplexing health problems and hoping that each of them in turn will help others with what they have learned. While I haven't "changed the world," I hope I have at least helped scores of people enrich their lives and by so doing, helped those with whom they come in contact.

8

Zinc: The Amazing Healer

When most people think of zinc, they think of a metal which is used to galvanize pipe and make brass and bronze. Rarely is zinc thought of as one of the most important healers of the human body. I have seen certain patients whose lives and personalities changed when zinc was supplied to their deficient tissues.

Zinc is an essential element in about eighty different enzymes which are necessary for proper functioning of the body. Enzymes are merely chemical "boosters" that speed up metabolic processes in the body. Zinc, like vitamins C and B, is used up much more quickly under conditions of stress. The more stress, the more zinc that is needed.

A very large percentage of the population is deficient in zinc because of the ingestion of so much refined and "junky" foods. It is estimated that 75 percent to 80 percent of all the zinc in grains is lost in the milling process. Much of the residue of the milling process is fed to animals. This is probably the reason we sometimes see world class animals being shown by unhealthy handlers. The animals are the healthy ones in this equation, and the consumer suffers. Don't ever fall for the advertising gimmick which seems to suggest that "enriched" flour is equal to or better than the whole unrefined product. In my opinion, enriched flour is merely enriched garbage that has been deodorized, and it should be considered as such.

Zinc is found in abundance in meats—especially livers—eggs, fish, nuts, beans, and whole grains. You will notice that some of these very valuable foods are the very foods your doctor is telling you are bad for your health. What a tremendous influence the food companies have had on the medical profession! All seafood provides fairly good quantities of zinc. The very richest source of zinc is found in oysters, which contain twenty-one times the amount found in some other meats. Probably less than half of the zinc in even good foods is capable of being utilized. That is even more reason why we should choose our foods wisely. In many patients, deficiencies have been built up over the years because the patient has eaten too much sugar and drunk too many soft drinks and too much alcohol. It is necessary to supplement the diet with additional zinc in such patients because sugar requires a lot of zinc for metabolism.

The following are some of the more common conditions that either can be caused by or abetted by a zinc deficiency.

- Lack of adequate ability to taste or smell.
- Inability to heal properly from a wound or disease.
- Dry, flaky, or cracking skin.
- Weak nails, especially those with white spots or white areas.
- Decreased immunity to infection or disease.
- Prostate problems such as infection or enlargement.
- Alopecia (loss of hair).

- Psoriasis. Such conditions need larger amounts of zinc.
- Repeated infections—especially ear and respiratory infections in children.
- Learning disabilities such as Attention Deficit Disorders and hyperactivity.
- Night blindness especially when combined with vitamin A deficiency.
- Stretch marks in the skin of the thighs and breasts.
- Nausea and vomiting during pregnancy. These problems are usually accompanied by a B6 deficiency.
- Retarded growth.
- Boils (furuncles).
- Eczema—often requires very large doses of zinc.
- Low sperm count in males.

The above are just some of the conditions in which zinc plays a very important role. The amount of zinc necessary to help these conditions varies greatly depending on the patient's problems, such as the state of digestive ability and the duration of the condition being treated. Also, it may be necessary to use zinc with other vitamins or minerals.

Over the years, I have seen some very impressive results with zinc supplementation. The cases are too numerous to recount, but a sampling may be of interest to you. One young lady immediately comes to mind. She had one of the most severe cases of acne I have ever seen. She was practically a recluse because of her self-consciousness. Correction of her diet and proper zinc supplementation changed her whole life.

Within six months, her skin had completely cleared and left almost no scarring. This young lady came out of her shell. She was happy in public and was having normal dating relationships with the opposite sex.

Many cases come to mind of babies who have had repeated ear infections and many who have had tubes in their ears (which in my opinion is another unproven medical fad and should rarely if ever be done). Within a few months of proper zinc supplementation and dietary correction, these babies became almost completely infection free. The results are often dramatic.

Although eczema is thought of as a skin disease, it is actually a metabolic disorder expressed by aggravating skin lesions. It is usually treated as a skin problem only, and underlying causes are seldom considered. This is a very stubborn health problem that requires extremely aggressive zinc supplementation (and other lifestyle corrections) and a lot of patience. The results can be rewarding. Furunculosis (repeated boils all over the body) responds dramatically to proper diet and zinc therapy. I recall a patient who had had boils for years which responded only temporarily to antibiotics. He was placed on an adequate diet and given large doses of zinc. Within a few months, his problem was completely gone.

I could go on and on about the many benefits of this very necessary mineral, but I wouldn't want you to get the idea that it is a "cure all." Like so many other very useful and important elements our bodies need, zinc works much more effectively if utilized with a good diet that eliminates certain factors that impair our health.

As I've mentioned before, I do my writing when I am in my little home in Alto Village (just north of Ruidoso, New Mexico). Here, in the peace and quiet amid the indescribable beauty around me, I seem to be better able to feel the real meaning of life and the presence of Him who has given me life. It makes me very sad to see the trend of activism and liberalism today that tries to teach our young people that respect for family and the love of God is outmoded and passe and that "alternative" lifestyles are normal and acceptable. I never in my wildest dreams ever imagined that I would live to see the day when the ruling authority in our government would advocate such things. I feel it is incumbent on those of us who have respect for God and family to speak up and try to set an example that demonstrates the wisdom of fundamental values.

Those of you who have been in my office must realize that I love good music—music that is relaxing and restful and easy on the ears. I think it enough of a traumatic experience just to go into a doctor's office with all of your doubts and uncertainties, without being subjected to a lot of the nerve wracking "music" on the radio. Good music can have a very relaxing and therapeutic effect, and I think it is very important for my patients to have a good feeling when they come to see me for their health. I select all of the music that is played in my office, and while I know that there is a lot of good music with meaningful words, I choose to play only instrumental music since I think it provides a more restful and enjoyable setting.

My favorite living vocalist is probably Perry Como. Although he is now about eighty years old, he still performs concerts and has a voice that is more mellow than ever. In 1987 he recorded a compact disc entitled Perry Como Today *which has many beautiful songs. The words in the last song of the CD should be our daily attitude. The song is entitled "The Best Of Times Is Now" and ends like this: "So hold this moment fast, and live and love as hard as you know how and make this moment last, because the best of times is now."*

9

Cholesterol: A Curse or a Life Saver?

A lot of what you are going to read in this chapter lends itself to much controversy and would, I am sure, be highly criticized by a good part of the medical profession and *all* of the pharmaceutical companies that make cholesterol-lowering drugs. However, my experience in the nutritional field and study of research published in very reliable medical journals, corroborates my thinking on this subject. I think you should know what I believe to be the truth.

I want to tell you a couple of stories to preface my remarks. The first happened some twenty or so years ago. One of the leading pharmaceutical companies came out with a new discovery—a cholesterol-lowering drug that was touted to be the cure-all for heart problems and arteriosclerosis (hardening of the arteries). It was given a broad reception in the medical community. Doctors were so brainwashed by the drug company that they immediately began prescribing the drug to many of their patients. The drug was called "Mer 29." Well, to make a long and sad story short, Mer 29 had been on the market only a very short time (about six months to a year as I remember), when many of these patients began to experience serious visual problems and general systemic problems from altered liver function. The trouble was traced to the drug Mer 29, and it was immediately removed from the market. Until the last few years, very little was heard about the necessity to lower cholesterol.

Now for the second story. A few years ago when the word "cholesterol" was still associated with good food and considered a valuable component of good health, the editor of the *Wall Street Journal* interviewed the president of one of the large drug companies. During their conversation, the editor was told that this drug company (and I will paraphrase his remarks) had discovered a wonderful new drug that would lower cholesterol levels, but the big problem was that they didn't have a market for it! Well, I'll bet you can guess the rest of the story. Multimillions of dollars have been spent in "educating" the medical profession, the FDA, the AMA, and the general public that cholesterol is the culprit causing heart attacks and that these new $2 pills would be the answer. Now you have seen the results of this massive advertising campaign. Doctors all over the country are putting patients on these new cholesterol-lowering drugs. There are several of them now. Many companies have gotten into the act.

The two stories sound very similar, don't they? The only difference is that the end of the second story has not yet been written. The rest of the story is now beginning to emerge after these drugs have been used for a few years. The harm that these drugs cause is being seen more and more and is being reported in some of our medical journals. I will quote some of them after I give you a little more information on cholesterol.

You are being led to believe that cholesterol is a bad word and that if you don't know "your number" you may be in danger of dying an early death. What you aren't being told is that "your number" can change very significantly from day to day or even hour to hour depending on many independent factors such as the time of day, fatigue, stress, food intake, and state of mind. You may be treated for a high cholesterol level which might not have been high if it had been taken at a different time or under different circumstances. I don't know "my number." I have never had it taken because I have no fear of cholesterol. If cholesterol is the *real cause* of heart attacks, why is it that more than 50 percent of heart attack victims have normal cholesterol levels? Also, if this cholesterol theory (and that's all it is—a theory) is true, how can it be that millions of people in their seventies and eighties have cholesterol readings above 250 and have no signs of arteriosclerosis?

Cholesterol is an absolutely essential substance in the body. The cell membranes of all the trillions of cells in the body are made of cholesterol. The hormones in our bodies are made of cholesterol. Much of our energy is converted from cholesterol. All the nerve sheaths are made of cholesterol. It is *not* true that the lower the cholesterol, the healthier the person. In fact, as you will read later in this article, lowering cholesterol by artificial means such as drugs, is causing a higher mortality rate than among those not treated! You don't read this in your newspapers or hear it from your friendly television doctors who just may have a vested interest in what they tell you.

The human body has to have an adequate amount of cholesterol to be healthy. If you don't eat it in such good foods as eggs, liver, and butter, your liver will manufacture it. Except in rare cases, which are attributed to genetic abnormalities, our bodies have an automatic mechanism in the liver that regulates the cholesterol level of the blood at any given time. Your cholesterol level may fluctuate as much as 50 percent or more depending on the amount of physical and mental stress you are under at the time your blood is drawn.

One of the principle functions of cholesterol is to protect our bodies during periods of stress. We may be doing the wrong thing to *artificially* lower our cholesterol level—nature may have elevated it for a reason. To illustrate this point, experiments have been done on race car drivers where their cholesterol levels were checked before and after a big race. The "before" levels could be perfectly normal, but the "after" readings were found to be increased by as much as 100 percent. The abnormal readings returned to normal when the unusual stress factor was no longer present.

Linus Pauling, biochemist and two-time Nobel prize winner, proved in his extensive research on this subject that high cholesterol levels of themselves are not harmful to health. It is only when the cholesterol sticks to the blood vessel walls that it becomes a problem. He also showed that it is the lack of certain nutrients that cause the vessel walls to become roughened and cracked so that the cholesterol can stick to the damaged vessel. As long as the vessel walls are slick and smooth, there can be no accumulation of cholesterol to cause clogging of the vessels and the consequent devastating effects.

Elevated cholesterol is merely a symptom of much deeper metabolic problems and should not be viewed as a cause. However, as is usual, the medical profession has been taught to treat symptoms and not causes. Hence all the hubbub over cholesterol levels. We have fallen into the trap of following the crowd, which is many times the wrong thing to do. Many physicians, like the drug companies, have been encouraging "cholesterol screenings," many of which have been proven to be as much as 50 percent inaccurate! A patient came into my office a few months ago who had been to a "free screening" at a local mall. She was told that her cholesterol level was 330 and that she should see her doctor immediately. She did as she was instructed, but before getting too excited, we did another test in a reliable laboratory and found the true reading to be 177. Before getting too paranoid about all the cholesterol propaganda, think about the economics of the situation.

One of the most well-known cardiologists of all time, Paul Dudley White (now deceased) said that before the turn of the century such things as heart attacks were virtually unknown. Yet, think of all the eggs, meat, and natural fats our forefathers ate. In the early part of this century, the average amount of sugar consumed per person was less than 20 pounds per year. This has gradually increased over the years until it is now about 120 pounds per person per year. In the early 1900s, there was almost no refining of flour, which removes most of its nutrients. Today, almost all flour is refined.

At the turn of the century, we were still eating natural fat foods. Now most of the fats we are ingesting are partially hydrogenated "low fat" foods which are being touted as better for us but in reality are killing us. Do we need to look further for the answers to the heart attack epidemic of today? Vitamins A, B, C, and E are known to protect against heart attacks. Many minerals like magnesium, calcium, and selenium have also been proven to protect, and yet this information has been largely withheld from the public. We must get back to more normal eating habits if we are to overcome the chronic diseases that plague us today!

The doctor's "drug bible" is the Physicians Desk Reference. It contains complete drug information on all drugs on the market. It is published annually. If you read the dangers, possible dangers, and precautions for most of the drugs being dispensed today, you would quake in your boots. Let me quote just a little bit about one of the major cholesterol-lowering drugs on the market. (I will not disclose the name of the particular drug since the warnings for all of them are about the same.) "———has been shown to reduce both normal and elevated LDL cholesterol concentrations. The effect of———induced changes in lipoprotein levels, including reduction of serum cholesterol, on cardiovascular morbidity or mortality *has not been established.*" (Emphasis is mine.)

Here we have a major industry, which makes billions of dollars from the sale of these drugs, telling physicians that it hasn't been proven to do any good. Now, isn't that dandy? It then goes on to warn physicians to do frequent liver tests to determine possible damage and that the damage caused may be irreversible. There are two pages of warnings and dangers for this particular drug, yet it is being used in wholesale quantities with very little attention to the warnings.

The October 1992 issue of *Medical World News* had a three-page article entitled "Lipid Controversy Builds Up." In it, some of the following things were written:

> "It has long been known; that too much cholesterol is not healthy for the heart, it now appears that too little cholesterol can have equally deleterious effects on the body's organs....Researchers have known since 1970 that low cholesterol was linked to an increase in hemorrhagic stroke, a finding first observed by the Japanese investigators who noticed a high rate of cerebral hemorrhage and low blood cholesterol in

> their country....Those with low cholesterol had two times the risk of dying of cerebral hemorrhage, five times the risk of dying from alcoholism, three times the risk of dying from liver cancer, and twice the risk of committing suicide....There is, however, a growing belief that the use of lipid-lowering drugs in low-risk populations whose only risk factor is high cholesterol may be ill advised."
>
> Well, what do you know about that?

The September 10, 1992, issue of *Medical Tribune* (now in its 34th year of publication) said: "There is no argument that an association between very low cholesterols and noncardiac mortality exists." Further in the article it says: "Low cholesterol levels are associated with up to a four fold greater risk of chronic obstructive lung disease."

In the October 1992 issue of *Hippocrates*, a medical journal, an article states: "The basic health message holds true, if someone is eating a good diet, to heck with cholesterol." Those are my sentiments exactly; however, you must know what constitutes a "good diet."

Please don't get the idea that I think unusually high cholesterol levels are normal or without harm. What I am trying to impress on you is that these levels are the result of other metabolic dysfunctions that need to be corrected and that cholesterol is merely taking the rap.

I never miss a chance to eat eggs, liver, nuts, and many of the other foods containing *natural* fats—along with plenty of the other good foods, of course—and plenty of vitamins and minerals. Maybe that is why I can still work and play sixteen hours a day and have no aches and pains. Think about it.

One piece of good news was published recently in a medical journal. Those who eat a handful of nuts daily have half the risk of heart attacks as those who don't. How can that be? Nuts contain fat, and current propaganda is telling us that fat is bad for our hearts. My comment would be: Of course nuts are good for us. They contain lots of good, essential fatty acids and a lot of magnesium and vitamin B6.

The other day I was listening to a medical program extolling the great advances in medical and drug therapy the past several years—most of which I didn't agree with—and it started me to thinking. I must have been born a contrarian. At least it seems so since I decided to go to medical school. I didn't have to choose the minority school of medicine (osteopathy) for my career. (Osteopathic physicians number less than 10 percent of the medical population.) I earned a scholarship for my first year in osteopathic college and could have chosen any medical school, M.D. or D.O., but I decided to be a D.O. because I thought the training offered for that degree equipped me with extra abilities for the betterment of my future patients (and I still think so).

During my schooling, I couldn't swallow all of the things that we were being taught about the use of drugs and I still can't. When I graduated and received my D.O. degree, many of the grads wanted to go to the big cities and many wanted to specialize. I wanted to be a general practitioner in a small town.

In my early years, tonsillectomies were the rage, and doctors would do them as a routine without medical justification. I abhorred the idea. Breast-feeding of newborns was laughed at as an archaic way to feed babies, and the pharmaceutical companies were successfully brainwashing doctors on the "health advantages" of formula feeding. I have always preached breast-feeding when at all possible.

Until a few years ago, the medical fad was to treat stomach ulcers with a cow's milk diet. I could never believe in it. Until recently the accepted medical treatment for treating hypoglycemia was to feed the patient frequent feedings of sweets (and some still do). This reasoning was always ridiculous to me.

Until a very few years ago, supplementation with vitamins was viewed by the majority of the medical profession as quackery (some still think so). I have believed and practiced vitamin and mineral therapy all of my practice life. The latest medical craze is cholesterol, and the majority of doctors have fallen right in line as they have been taught to do. I have never believed all this propaganda.

10

Fat: Evil Killer or God-Made Necessity?

This chapter is one of the most difficult I have attempted to write. In previous chapters, I have tried to make you aware of what I believe to be the real truth about some controversial subjects. For more than sixty years, the public, and yes, even of the medical community has been brainwashed about fats. To speak contrary to the dictates of "accepted knowledge" would almost seem to be the same as speaking against motherhood. However, I believe the stakes are so high and the damage being done so great, that I want you to know what I believe to be the truth on this subject. The food companies are the activists, and the food companies and the medical profession are the benefactors. The public, as usual, is the victim.

Fats are a very complicated subject. For the purpose of this book, however, we will think of them as the greasy substances found in meat, eggs, vegetable oils, and milk. Cholesterol and triglycerides are fat-like substances that are taking a lot of the blame for conditions for which they are not responsible. The body cannot exist without an adequate amount of fat. We can be in real trouble if at least 25 percent to 30 percent of our calories do not come from good fats.

Fats are our most concentrated source of energy. They have four times the energy potential of carbohydrates. Every cell in our bodies is made of fat in the form of cholesterol. From it the body manufactures hormones and vitamin D. The liver and brain manufacture from 1,500 to 2,000 mg. of cholesterol daily to insure proper functioning of the body. Cholesterol acts as a lubricant for healthy arteries. As the old cells wear out, the HDL (good cholesterol) carries them to the liver for elimination while the LDL (so-called bad cholesterol) brings new cholesterol for the manufacture of new cells. It is a natural continuing process of nature to keep our blood vessels in good shape and to keep them from clogging up. So how can natural fats and cholesterol be so bad? They aren't; but notice I emphasize *natural fats*.

Reason would lead us to believe that if natural fats killed us humans, Eskimos would have been a vanishing race before we took Alaska into the United States since they lived on nothing but whale blubber. However, the Eskimos didn't start dying of heart attacks until several years later, after they had partaken of our refined sugar and flour foods and our "better for you" transformed fat foods. So, logic would lead us to believe that natural fats are not the cause of the many diseases for which they are being blamed.

Those of you who are old enough to remember the great depression of the 1930s will remember that your mother used to buy white margarine which came with a little packet of orange dye powder. It could be mixed with the margarine so that it would look like butter. It became quite popular because it was cheaper than butter, and money was a very scarce commodity in those days. The food companies told us that it was just as good as butter. We believed them then as we still do. Surely the big food companies would not sell us something that was bad for our health. What they were selling us was a new fat called partially hydrogenated fat. Another name is trans fatty acid. These new fats were made by heating an otherwise good vegetable oil to destroy its odor and then bubbling hydrogen through it to make it firm (like butter).

Probably, at the time of its inception, research had not been as extensive as it has been since. Maybe the food companies didn't realize what damage this new type of fat would do to the health of the people who ate it. We will give them the benefit of the doubt. However, over the past sixty years or so, vast quantities of research has been done which reveals that the trans fatty acids are at the root of many of our health problems—including heart disease and cancer.

Trans fatty acids, or partially hydrogenated fats, are known to interfere with the manufacture of prostaglandins, which are responsible for many vital metabolic functions in our body. Since this type of fat is foreign to the body, the body doesn't know how to digest and utilize it. Partly because of the problems caused by the ingestion of trans fats, the blood vessels lose their elasticity and become roughened on the inside. The consequent collection of particles of cholesterol and calcium begin to form on the inside of the vessel. In a number of years, these particles block the vessel entirely and a heart attack occurs. Since cholesterol is present in the vessel, it gets the blame when actually it had no part in the real cause of the damaged blood vessel. In this way, the partially hydrogenated fats can be the cause of many of the degenerative diseases prevalent today. These abnormal fats do not contain the essential fatty acids that are natural to the human body.

The best sources of the essential fatty acids are *unheated* and *unrefined* flaxseed oil, canola oil, and olive oil. Fats found in natural foods such as eggs, nuts, avocados, meats, and *unaltered* dairy products do not create a utilization problem for the human body. It is not the fats themselves that are detrimental to our health but the damage that is being done to them for the sake of profit. Partially hydrogenated fats are cheaper to make and keep longer on the shelf and that spells more bucks. You ask "if these products are so injurious to our health why doesn't the FDA—the so called protector of the people—do something about it?" The reason should be quite obvious. The "Golden Rule:" the one who has the gold makes the rules. The artificial fat business is a multi-billion dollar business, and the FDA would far rather spend its time trying to take vitamins off the market than to interfere with the sale of these dangerous trans fats.

In early 1994, the story broke all over television and newspapers that butter was much better for your health than margarine. They told about the extensive research that validated their story. They also told about the partially hydrogenated or trans fats. You will also recall that after about two days you did not see or read anymore about this scandalous insult to the health of the people of the United States. The multimillions of dollars that the food companies spend in television and newspaper advertising every year allows them to enforce the "Golden Rule."

Partially hydrogenated fats are found in *all* margarines. Margarine accounts for about 7 percent of all the dietary fat intake of the average person in this country. Don't be fooled by advertising. So, it has no cholesterol. So what? Vegetable oils never did have any cholesterol. Only animal products contain cholesterol. *Don't eat margarine!* Eat real old-fashioned butter!

Almost all of the fast-food chains use partially hydrogenated fats in their products. Almost all packaged baked goods are made with the trans fats. Look on almost any package you buy, and you will see that it lists "partially hydrogenated oil" as the fat ingredient. Don't eat the products advertised as "low fat" this and "low fat" that. They are made with the bad fats. Don't eat the man-made fats. Eat only natural fats and have no fear. Stick to my old rule: "If God made it, eat it. If man made it, don't."

It is tragically ironic that some of the very foods we are told to eat to protect our health are the very foods that are sending us to the coronary care units in droves. If you don't learn anything else from this chapter remember that heart attacks and clogged blood vessel problems didn't begin in this country with any regularity until the advent of refined flour and sugar and the consumption of man-made partially hydrogenated fats. With increasing consumption of these products, encouraged by massive media advertising, almost all chronic health problems have increased in like proportion. To those who are genuinely interested in their health and well-being, I need not say more.

It's great to be alive! I don't mean just to be conscious and breathing—I mean to feel good and enjoy to its fullest the life that we have been given. The longer I live and the more I see, the more I realize that a large percentage of the population is metabolically alive but not really living. Health is the key to really living. If we don't have health, life becomes more of a burden than a joy. I see so many people who, because of poor health, cannot enjoy their most wonderful possession—life.

Health can be such a simple thing if we would only open our eyes and use our common sense. It doesn't take a medical education to be healthy. In fact, statistics show that doctors are right near the top of the list for suicides, and healthy, happy people don't commit suicide! Higher education is not a prerequisite for health, but common sense is.

In most cases, health is such an attainable thing. I realize that there are genetic factors which can cause poor health, but these factors are greatly in the minority. Even they can many times be influenced for good by proper living habits. How much of the time we miss "living" because of our poor choices, committed either because of ignorance or lack of will. How many times I see people who are not really living because they "just don't feel good." It is very easy for doctors to tell patients to "get a grip on themselves" but it is impossible for people to do that when they have a real health problem which is the basis for the way they are feeling and thinking. Happy thinking is not something that you can will yourself to do if the physical brain is not chemically healthy. Health and happiness is the normal condition for human beings. Disease and unhappiness is generally caused by things we do to ourselves!

But, you say, if health is a simple thing to attain, why do I still feel bad after going to so many doctors? The question is good; the answer is difficult. Most doctors are trained to recognize specific diseases which are characterized by specific symptoms. Unfortunately, we are not trained to teach our patients health. *Hence, most doctors are satisfied to treat symptoms. In some cases, the treatment of symptoms is all that is needed, but too often the real cause of the symptoms is not considered.*

11

Antibiotics: Too Much of a Good Thing

A good friend sent me an article he had seen in the September 1994 issue of *Fortune* magazine. I urge all of you to get that issue and read the article entitled "Killer Microbes." This article recounts what I have been telling my patients for years—that antibiotics are a mixed blessing and should be used much more cautiously and less frequently. Certainly, this is not the first nor will it be the last you will hear about the fears of the Government Center for Disease Control and the medical profession about the overwhelming number of different types of bacteria which have become resistant to antibiotic therapy.

These bacteria have become resistant because antibiotics have been used so indiscriminately for so many years. Some of the scientists in the biology labs that make antibiotics say that almost all disease-causing bacteria are evolving toward complete resistance. And the dangerous and pitiful part of it is that there seems to be nothing science has yet found to do about it. This article points out that a single microbe can produce ten to twenty million offspring in a single day! As a result, the resistant strains are evolving with ever increasing speed.

The article in *Fortune* magazine is not the only warning we have been seeing on this subject. The September 1, 1994, issue of *Family Practice News* devotes much of the issue to the fact that antibiotics are losing the war against resistant bacteria. It tells how doctors are using far too many antibiotics even when they feel that they may be of limited or no value. They are also being used for too long a period of time. If they haven't done any good in four or five days, they probably won't help. Yet, how many times have you been given a prescription and told to take it for the full ten days or two weeks or longer without bothering to check to see if the antibiotic is helping? Patients must realize that they also must have some responsibility for their own health. You can't run to the doctor with every little sore throat or runny nose. The doctor feels that he must do something or you wouldn't think he is earning his fee, so he gives you an antibiotic. It's the accepted and easy thing to do even though it isn't going to do any good and in fact, may possibly do harm.

Of course, you and I know that the proper way to overcome infection is *not* by creating more and better antibiotics but by getting and maintaining a healthy immune system that will let nature take care of the bacteria. Most patients in hospitals have very impaired immune systems and provide fertile breeding grounds for the bacteria that are present in all hospitals. That is one reason why I try to keep my patients out of hospitals.

As I have emphasized many times to my patients, the answer to health is not antibiotics and medicines but rather learning how to attain a lifestyle which includes plenty of good, unprocessed foods with plenty of fiber, natural fats, plenty of God-given liquids, adequate amounts of exercise, establishment of complete daily bowel habits, and lots of thankfulness for the joy of life. If we do these things, most illness will become a thing of the past and most medicines will not be necessary!

If I could adequately describe what I have just seen, you would be better able to understand the tranquility I feel when I am in this "little nest in the mountains." Let me try to paint you a verbal picture. It is nine o'clock in the evening and the moon is about as full as it can get. The temperature outside is a crisp twenty-eight degrees. I have just returned from a walk up the steep incline of the road in front of my house where I can look down and see the lights of the cozy warmth inside and the smoke gently rising from the chimney. My eyes follow the road down past the house and then turn upward and to the left to see the full moon brilliance of the snow-covered Sierra Blanca peak. My ears strain to hear a sound—any sound at all—but there is none. Absolute silence prevails. The beauty is so breathtaking and the aura so penetrating that I wish every one of you could experience the ultimate peace that I am feeling at this moment. Is it any wonder that I love to write in this setting?

Hopefully, the chapters you have read already have given you enough knowledge to allow you to assume some responsibility for your own health and to see your health problems in a new light. We doctors cannot be responsible for your health and well-being. We should only be your teachers, present at times of necessity in order to show you how to correct mistakes that you may have made, resulting in your ill feeling. The more we can teach you, the less dependent you become on us. That is as it should be. Unfortunately, that is not the way the framers of medical opinion want you to think.

So much of the modern teaching for the treatment of disease is contrary to my personal convictions and that of the osteopathic concept. The body has within itself the ability to cure most of its own health problems if only given the proper environment (both mechanical and nutritional). In most branches of the medical professions, this type of thinking is entirely foreign to what doctors have been taught. It is no wonder that we spend most of our time patching up an unhealthy body with temporary measures while the patient continues the lifestyle that makes the return to our office inevitable. Maybe someday it will be different.

Up to this point, the chapters of this book have described a single substance, vitamin, or mineral and how that knowledge can be utilized for the improvement of your health. The remainder of the book will be devoted to a more "cookbook" approach to the nutritional treatment of various conditions that I see frequently in the office.

Please keep in mind when you are reading these suggestions that I am not trying to treat people who are not under my care. That could be a dangerous thing to do for certain conditions without proper diagnosis. However, as I mentioned above, I think people should take much more responsibility for their own health and it is in this vein that this information should be utilized—definitely not to countermand the orders of any other doctor.

I believe that most health problems are quite simple. Even some of the most incapacitating problems have simple solutions but take more intense effort and a longer period of time to correct.

12

Odds and Ends You Can Take to the Bank #1

This chapter (and two more to follow) is devoted to conditions that I see in the office on a daily basis—things that are quite bothersome. Patients seek medical help for these conditions, often to no avail. Some have spent thousands of dollars and come up with no answers.

Please keep in mind that the following suggestions may be only the most important things that can be done for the condition under consideration and that other things would also be of value but would make too detailed a discussion for this book. Also keep in mind that all of these conditions have probably been brought on over the years by poor diet and that the diet must be corrected as emphasized in all of my previous chapters.

Leg Cramps

Generally speaking, chronically occurring leg cramps have a simple solution. Actually, I should include any kind of muscle cramping because I can recall many patients with disabling back cramps and muscle cramps in other parts of the body. Usually, adequate calcium *and* magnesium intake will correct this problem.

The use of calcium alone is sometimes not effective at all. The utilization of calcium is dependent to a large degree on an adequate amount of magnesium. Many people have the mistaken idea that drinking milk will solve the problem, but it doesn't. In fact, some of the worst cases of muscle cramping I have encountered have been in people who drink large amounts of milk.

It seems ironic that pasteurized cow's milk, which is touted to supply us with plenty of calcium, sometimes actually makes cramping worse. Pasteurization destroys the phosphatase in milk and makes milk somewhat indigestible. Also, as we become adults we lose the ability to produce the lactase which is necessary to metabolize the sugar (lactose) in milk. As a consequence, milk often becomes an indigestible substance which causes a lot of stomach trouble, sinus problems, and allergies.

Usually about 1,000 to 1,200 mg. of calcium and about 500 to 600 mg. of magnesium each day will relieve the muscle cramps in a few days to a few weeks. Sometimes vitamin E complex in fairly large doses is also required. Occasionally, moderate doses of potassium are needed. I see so many people taking drugs to alleviate this problem when these simple solutions are a lot less expensive and a lot safer.

Spontaneous Bruising

One of the most common problems I see in the office is black and blue marks on the arms and legs when there has been no trauma to cause them. These patients are usually taking certain drugs, that if taken long enough, will certainly break down the blood vessels in the skin and the bruise marks result. Long-term use of prednisone (cortisone), aspirin, or almost any of the anti-inflammatory drugs cause this problem. We are told that aspirin is a "wonder drug." This is far from the truth. Continued use of aspirin has numerous and potentially serious side effects. The blood thinning benefits of aspirin can be had by taking vitamin E with no side effects.

The way to overcome spontaneous bruising is to stop taking the offending drug if possible. Some should be stopped only under the guidance of a doctor. The patient should then take vitamin C (2,000 to 4,000 mg.), bioflavinoids (1,000 to 2,000 mg.), and vitamin E (400 to 800 units) daily. It may take several months to strengthen the blood vessels before you see a definite change.

Tachycardia (Spells of rapid heartbeat)

Tachycardia is a common problem. People spend thousands of dollars on various methods of diagnosis, some of which have potentially dangerous side effects. This is one of the simplest things to correct. Many times the problem is caused by some medication the patient is taking. In any case, the answer is generally found in a five-cent 300 mg. or 400 mg. magnesium tablet taken two or three times a day. Magnesium has an important role in controlling the mechanism which controls the heart rate and rhythm. You must keep in mind that magnesium also has a laxative effect if too large a quantity is taken. That quantity varies from person to person.

Mitral Valve Prolapse

Mitral valve prolapse has become a dumping ground diagnosis on which to blame every ache and pain in the chest or every skipped heartbeat or spell of tachycardia which the doctor cannot explain. The majority of problems blamed on mitral valve prolapse are actually not caused by it. It is only since the advent of echocardiagrams that we have been able to diagnose mitral valve prolapse. Many patients have had it for years and didn't know it but now that it can be diagnosed, it is a dump ground for our ignorance in most cases. Other reasons will generally be found to explain symptoms now blamed on mitral valve prolapse.

A lot of the things that I write about and describe to you may not have much direct bearing on your health. They are, however, things that come to mind at odd moments during the day or when I sit down to write that I think may help you to appreciate and enjoy life a little more. After all, that is what this book is all about.

As I sit on the deck observing the scenery in my usual spot, I am listening to the sweet, soft, melodious strains of "Dreams and Memories" as only Perry Como can sing it. The temperature on this midwinter day is fifty-five degrees and the sun is shining brightly in a perfectly clear blue sky. Just a little distance up the hill a mother deer with her two little fawns is searching for food and eating some of the green leaves off the tree branches. I am reminded that in spite of all the earthquakes, blizzards, floods, and turmoil in the world, there is still a lot of peace and harmony in nature if we will only take time to see it.

I read a book a couple of months ago that I would recommend to everyone. It was written by the late Arthur Ashe and is titled "Days of Grace." It was his last work before he died, and the last chapters were written when he knew that death was impending. He had so many reasons to feel that the "deck was stacked against him" and yet he emerged as one of America's most admired people. Through all the years he lived in the public eye as one of the best professional tennis players that ever lived and also as an impassioned proponent of his race, he was never known to be anything but a perfect gentleman worthy of emulation. One thing he said in the book that stuck in my memory was, (and I'm paraphrasing) that if he could put an asset value on personal characteristics, his reputation would be his most valuable asset. How true that is in personal dealings or in business. Your reputation follows you for a lifetime. If it is trustworthy, it can open many doors and if it is not, it can ruin your life.

I saw a refrigerator magnet the other day that provoked a lot of thought. It read: "The best things in life are not things." I started to think of all the characteristics people exhibit that make our lives pleasant but are not "things." A smile was the first thing that came to mind. Did you know that it is impossible to worry when you are smiling? Even when we feel bad, the very act of smiling often and sincerely can help to make a bad situation better for the one who is smiling as well as for others to whom the smile is directed.

13

Odds and Ends You Can Take to the Bank #2

Repeated Ear Infections in Children

This is generally a problem caused by *too much* antibiotic treatment. These children are generally eating far too many sweets, drinking too many soft drinks, and taking repeated antibiotics, all of which suppress the immune system. Putting tubes in the ears *is not* the answer. The answer is to correct the diet and give plenty of natural foods, vitamin C (1,000 mg. to 2,000 mg. per day—and not just when sick), and zinc. I call zinc the healing mineral because it is so necessary in all healing processes. A small infant can take 10 mg. a day and a two or three year old can take 20 mg. without danger. More and more of the medical literature is telling doctors not to use repeated antibiotics for ear infections and not to resort to so much ear tubing. These things are hard to stop because of the economics of the thing, but think about the poor child.

Most of these children who have had repeated antibiotics over a period of several months to several years are victims of systemic yeast problems—a diagnosis in which most doctors don't put much credence. However, the real chronic ear infection problems can generally be overcome in a few weeks or months by adding the yeast killing medicine Nystatin to the treatment. The use of antibiotics for the treatment of ear infections may sometimes still be necessary, but it should be used more judiciously than is now the practice. You should seek the advice of a doctor schooled in nutrition for the treatment of this problem.

Chronic Prostate Infection and/or Enlargement

Chronic prostate infection and/or enlargement can be caused by many things. Three of the most common are constipation, lack of exercise, and inadequate emptying of the seminal fluid via ejaculation. Zinc is essential to the health of the prostate gland. Saw palmetto berries or extract is also helpful.

Fever Blisters (Herpes Simplex)

There have been many drugs and rub-on preparations used in the treatment of the very annoying and painful condition of fever blisters. The trouble is that most of them don't work.

The cause of the problem is apparently a virus (but then viruses are always the cause of conditions that we have trouble curing). The real cause is more basic than that. Viruses may be present, but the basic problem is that the skin has lost its inherent immunity to protect itself against the invasion of the virus.

Experience has taught me that there may be several factors present before fever blisters develop. Usually there is a history of a large intake of sugar in one form or another and the usual culprit is soft drinks—regular or diet, it makes no difference. There also appears to be an upset in the arginine to lysine ratio in the blood. Arginine is richly abundant in foods that contain chocolate. Again, too much sweet stuff!

Fever blisters also are frequently found after antibiotics have been taken for an infection. The antibiotics wipe out the normal bacteria (acidophilus) in the bowel which serve to protect against various invaders.

Common sense would then tell us that the answer to this problem is quite simple. Eliminate the sugar and chocolate foods from the diet and take lots of lysine (a naturally occurring amino acid). Take plenty of vitamin C. I sometimes prescribe as much as 3,000 mg. of lysine daily on an empty stomach and several thousand mg. of vitamin C. Take acidophilus and be careful about taking antibiotics for every little illness. Let the body fight some for itself. Antibiotics weaken the immune system and should be used with respect.

I recall a male patient who came to me about two or three years ago. He was thirty-three years old and had mouth ulcers and fever blisters so bad for the last twelve years that he was unable to chew most foods or tolerate any fruits or juices because of the pain. His mouth and lips were completely covered with sores. He had been through a lot of anguish trying to find help. All kinds of specialists, drugs, and treatments had been tried to no avail. The man was obviously malnourished and had lost a lot of weight.

The amazing thing to me about his previous care was that not one of the doctors he had encountered asked him *anything* about his diet. Analysis of his eating habits revealed a huge sugar and chocolate intake with several cans of a popular soft drink daily. Correction of his diet and implementation of the above mentioned treatment began to show immediate results. Within three months this patient had no more mouth ulcers or fever blisters.

He came to see me about a year later for another problem, and he was still free of his fever blisters. Another victory for good, simple, and sensible nutritional care.

Although in all probability more than three quarters of my life is over, I feel like a very lucky person. I'll bet if a lot of you want to take time to analyze it, you will feel the same way and maybe for a lot of the same reasons. I was fortunate in my "choice" of parents. They instilled in me a strong belief in God and what I hope is an acceptable set of moral standards. They taught me a strong work ethic that has served me well and helped me to realize that nothing that comes without effort is worthwhile.

I have been extremely blessed with a wonderful wife who has stuck with me through the hard times and the good times and has been the stabilizing influence in my life. I have five wonderful children who have been nothing but a source of joy. I often tell Lynne that I feel our greatest accomplishment in this life has been our children. I couldn't possibly leave out the eleven grandchildren and two great grandchildren (with another on the way). What a source of pride and joy which has made all the hard work and sweat worthwhile. All of the above are the things in life of which I am the most proud.

There is another principle reason why I feel that I am a very lucky man. I have my health. Although this is certainly good fortune, I do not think of it as entirely "luck." I feel very fortunate that circumstances of my life guided me into the practice of nutritional healing approximately twenty-five years ago. Since that time, I have been continually learning how to take care of not only my patients, but myself. Without my change of lifestyle, I probably would not be around to help you with your problems and have the opportunity to write this book. I practice the things that I am constantly preaching to you. So now you may understand why I awake every morning thanking God for one more beautiful day of life.

Earlier in the book, I said that "the best things in life are not things." How about the feeling you get when you have gone that "extra mile" to help someone who is in need of your particular skills. The feeling is certainly something you cannot measure except by the warm feeling it gives you inside.

14

Odds and Ends You Can Take to the Bank #3

Cervical Dysplasia

Cervical dysplasia is a very common problem among women who have taken birth control pills for any length of time or for women who have had a poor diet over a period of many years. This problem often results in a Pap smear which shows some atypical or inflammatory cells. Much surgery is done on such cervical tissue in the form of freezing and conizations (surgical removal of the inflamed tissue). In my estimation, there is generally a much less costly and more natural way of correcting the condition if it hasn't already advanced to the stage of cervical cancer. Birth control pills contain estrogen and progesterone and women taking them require a lot more of certain vitamins and minerals to protect against the adverse effects of the extra hormones. Among those most necessary are daily doses of folic acid (5 to 10 mg.), zinc (50 to 100 mg.), vitamin C (2,000 to 3,000 mg.), and vitamin A (50,000 I.U. from fish liver oil) for a month or two with professional monitoring, preferably from a doctor who is nutritionally oriented.

Bell's Palsy

Bell's palsy is a very disturbing condition that is often mistaken for a stroke. Bell's palsy is progressive paralysis of one side of the face. Many times it occurs after a serious stress, either emotional or physical. The condition generally responds to niacin (100 mg.) after each meal. Be prepared to encounter the harmless flush that often follows ingestion of niacin. It only lasts about thirty minutes or so and usually for only a few days. Then, the body gets used to the niacin and the "flush" becomes minimal. The reaction is harmless—in fact, beneficial—and should not be a matter of concern. Vitamin B complex (50 mg.) also should be taken twice daily. Vitamin B12 injections of 1,000 mg. daily for ten consecutive days is sometimes helpful. A response is usually seen in one to three weeks, with progressive improvement thereafter.

Kidney Stones

Kidney stones are a very painful condition which result when small accumulations of calcium oxalate try to pass through the small ureter tube that leads from the kidney to the bladder.

In spite of the fact that these small stones usually contain calcium, they are *not* caused by excessive calcium intake. Limiting or excluding calcium from the diet, as if often suggested, will not cure the condition. Improper calcium utilization is the cause. Since magnesium is necessary to utilize calcium, magnesium is of prime importance (500 to 1,000 mg.). It alone, however, will not prevent the formation of excessive oxalic acid which combines with the calcium. Vitamin B6 is necessary for the proper metabolism of oxalic acid and must be given in adequate quantities (100 to 300 mg.). Vitamin A (25,000 I.U.) must also be given. Meat intake should be lowered since excessive meat consumption increases the urinary excretion of calcium. Sugar intake must be stopped or drastically curtailed since sugar increases the production of insulin, which in turn causes excess calcium excretion through the kidney.

I recall a case I had several years ago. A man in his thirties was passing kidney stones every week or so and besides the pain it was causing, the expense of surgically removing them was becoming prohibitive. I put him on the program shown above. Within a week, he was passing no more stones and did not form any more stones as long as he was taking adequate amounts of magnesium and B6 and remained on a good diet.

Restless Legs

Restless legs is a very annoying condition in which it seems the legs must always be moving. It is sometimes accompanied by muscular discomfort and cramping. It is especially noticeable at night when interference with sleep is noticed. Improvement is frequently noticed in just a few days with magnesium (500 to 1,000 mg.), calcium (1,000 to 1,200 mg.), vitamin E (400 to 800 units), and folic acid (5 mg.).

Vitiligo

Vitiligo is a very distressing and progressive loss of pigment in the skin. Most vitiligo patients have a lack of hydrochloric acid (HCl) in the stomach and hence cannot break down their protein foods well. Some have no hydrochloric acid at all. It is therefore necessary to furnish five or ten grains of betaine HCl tablets just before each meal. PABA (para amino benzoic acid) is very essential. It is a part of the vitamin B complex and is used in doses of 200 to 400 mg. twice daily. Vitamin B complex (50 mg. once or twice a day). Brewer's yeast is very beneficial also since it is a good source of B vitamins, protein, lecithin, and minerals. This condition responds very slowly but improvement can be expected to start in a few months. It may take a year or two for satisfactory repigmentation.

I had a humbling experience last month. I was in Midland, Texas playing in the Southwest Oilman's Tennis Tournament. Although this tournament is restricted to oil business personnel, I am allowed to play because I have two sons, Craig and Gary, in the oil business and I act as the tournament physician. The rules dictate that if you get to the finals in your division the previous year, you are automatically placed in the next higher bracket the next year. So, I found myself in the Championship division this year (where I don't belong) playing against some of the best young players in Texas. I was soundly beaten. They put this old man in his place.

After the tournament, I had a couple of days before going back to the office. I decided to drive on down to San Antonio. Three of my children, Carol, Craig, and Gary, live there. My youngest son, David, was entered in a United States Tennis Association tournament there, so I could "kill two birds with one stone." David is a championship grade tennis player and I dearly love to watch him play. I continue to learn how the game should be played.

If you have ever driven the 100-mile stretch between Midland, Texas, south to Interstate 10, you realize that there is a tremendous amount of spacious and open country where even an automobile is rarely encountered. The openness of the country creates a certain exhilarating awe which I always feel when viewing the vastness of God's creation. It provided a lot of time to think.

To anyone with a competitive spirit who strives for a certain level of excellence, a sound whipping now and then is a good thing. It stimulated a lot of thought processes. Even in my younger days, was I ever as good as those kids who just beat me? I doubt it. I know that I was never as good as David, who I would be watching shortly. I also know that at my age, no matter how hard I try, I won't be able to reach that level of expertise. However, that doesn't stop me from trying to improve. When we quit trying to improve ourselves, no matter what our age or what our endeavor, we might as well die.

It grieves me that the achievement of excellence in education is no longer the goal of the lawmakers of this nation for its young people. It is so wrong to encourage lazy and lascivious behavior under the guise of "self-expression." While many individual teachers would love to see excellence and achievement thrive, they are greatly hampered by the regulations under which they are forced to teach. Rather than the pursuit of individual accomplishment, we are slowly beginning to accept the oft repeated populist theory that laziness and dependence should be rewarded at the expense of excellence and achievement. The sad result of this type of thinking will be to reduce all young people to a mediocre level rather than to raise the abilities of the underachievers.

In a way, the medical profession has fallen into this same type of thinking. Instead of educating and encouraging patients to attain better levels of health by expending effort to do the things that have to be done to improve their health, many physicians take the lazy road and assume that most patients will be satisfied if their symptoms can merely be controlled with one drug or another. Physicians disregard their reason for existence—teaching patients how to achieve true health.

I guess within all of us there lurks that sinister laziness which is willing to accept the status quo rather than to expend effort and energy to improve. Those who accept this type of thinking will never be truly satisfied with what they have achieved. They will always wonder what it would have been like to experience life from the next higher rung on the ladder. No matter what our station in life or our abilities, the desire to achieve and to improve should be the driving force that keeps us relatively young and active and looking forward to tomorrow.

15

Raising Healthy Children

Most of the patients in my practice are adults. They present themselves to me with a wide variety of illnesses and health problems that are generally found in adults. Adults have had a long time to abuse their bodies with a multiplicity of bad habits which culminate in disease. However, many of my patients are parents who have young children, and they express an interest in raising their children in a healthy manner so as to help them eliminate much unnecessary illness and escape the ravages of future health problems. I have become aware of the fact that many patients who are grandparents are sharing much of this nutritional knowledge with their children in order to help their grandchildren. Since it is my ultimate desire to *prevent* disease problems in my patients as well as their children, I think a chapter on raising healthy children is apropos.

Actually, the general principles of *preventing* illness in youngsters are essentially the same as *curing* illness in adults. Fortunately, it is much easier since the little ones have not had as much time as adults to become victims of today's harmful lifestyles and eating habits.

I do not hesitate to say that at least 75 percent of all the illness in children is unnecessary. Parents are responsible for a lot of that 75 percent. Most of the respiratory infections, sore throats, asthma, hyperactivity, attention deficit problems, ear infections, and skin problems are a direct result of malnutrition!

When we hear the word malnutrition, we immediately visualize the skinny, starving children we see nightly on television. That is truly a tragedy for which human wisdom apparently has no answer. Malnutrition, however, is not necessarily starvation. It is merely poor nutrition from which a large percentage of children suffer. What a paradox. We live in a land where food is abundant, where most people eat two or three times as much as their bodies require, and yet, have diseases caused by malnutrition. Not too many people involved in "health care" today will agree with me, but that is precisely why there is the need for so much disease care in this country. If physicians provided real health care, this paradox would not exist.

Most children who get sick frequently do so because their little bodies do not have the necessary nutrients to furnish their immune systems with the ammunition it takes to defeat the causative factors of disease. It is that simple. It then should seem to be common sense that if we furnish our children with the appropriate nutrients, they will get well and remain well most of the time.

Living in today's society, perfect health is not possible. But optimal health is possible, and it should be easier for our children because until a certain age, these little people are captives to our nurturing. We can see that they get only those things that will produce healthy bodies and freedom from disease! It is in the formative years that we should instill in children the knowledge of what is good and what is bad. This certainly should apply to foods as well as morality. As they get older, children will be confronted with all the bad lifestyles and nutritional habits to which we are all subject, but at least they will have a firm foundation on which to build. That is certainly more than a lot of kids are getting today!

Recall from Chapter 1 my observations on how we are raised to be sugar addicts from the time we are born. It is from this time that the ingestion of refined sugar begins to weaken the immune systems of the little ones. It begins with sugar water in the nursery, soft drinks in nursing bottles, sugared baby foods, and sugared cereals. Then come candy treats and Halloween goodies. It goes on and on and gets worse as they get older. Also, as they get older, they become the advertising targets of junk food companies. Then, peer pressure begins to raise its ugly head. Unless children have a solid foundation of knowledge about eating for good health, and unless they also *learn by example*, how can they be expected to escape the ravages of poor nutrition and the consequent illness that it brings?

A healthy child can be expected to come from a healthy mother and father who have seen to it that the child has been conceived with healthy ovum and sperm. The child should also have adequate nutrition while in the womb.

I believe breast-feeding is very important. Mother's milk is made for human babies and cows milk is made for calves. It is that simple. In cases of necessity, cow's milk can be altered in baby formulas to serve the purpose, but it is never optimal.

A large percentage of babies are allergic to cow's milk and it doesn't necessarily show up in skin tests. In my estimation and that of many other nutritionally oriented physicians, pasteurized cow's milk is not a good food for children or adults. Certainly, no asthmatic child should even look at milk. Ideally, a child should be breast-fed for six months to a year.

Usually, breast milk alone is adequate for at least six months. During this time, small amounts of diluted pure fruit juice can be given along with adequate amounts of pure water (not chlorinated tap water). At four to six months of age, small amounts of fruits, vegetables, eggs, and whole grain cereals can be added if necessary to control hunger greater than breast milk can satisfy. These foods can be ground up in a baby food grinder from fresh foods or *unsugared* baby foods can be given. Then, the children gradually grow into table foods. This is where parental example begins to be very important.

During these early months, a dropper of a good children's vitamin is very important just for insurance if nothing else. Vitamin C is very important to establish a strong immune system. A small baby who is breast-feeding may get enough vitamin C if the mother's supply is adequate. However, as the baby gets to be a few months old, it is a good health practice to give the baby 500 mg. a day. This can be done by putting a little vitamin C powder in a small amount of diluted fruit juice or as liquid vitamin C that can be given in a dropper. These can be obtained at any health food store. My final general suggestion on illness prevention in babies and children is the old-fashioned habit of giving all babies a dropper of cod liver oil every day.

If babies are breast-fed; kept away from cow's milk, all sugared drinks, and sugared baby foods; given children's vitamins, vitamin C, and cod liver oil; most of the childhood infections will be avoided.

For most of us, the way we think of ourselves has a great deal to do with the kind of person we are. Most of us also appraise situations and judge normality in very relative terms—almost always relative to our own experiences or to ourselves. Let me give you an example that I got a big kick out of. The other day, I had a patient in my office who was more than ninety years of age. Although in good health for his age (a relative term), he was admitting to a few of the afflictions of age. During our conversation, he asked me: "Say, how old are you anyway?" I told him I was seventy-four years old. He said in a jovial tone: "I knew you were just a kid the way you jump around the office." I thought I was getting up there in years, but to him I was "just a kid."

After work that day, I got to thinking about what he had said. It impressed upon me a fact that I had never stopped to really think about before. Most of our judgments and decisions and most of what wisdom we have gained is based upon our own life experiences and whom and what we believe ourselves to be. It is very frightening to think that many of the decisions based upon such a precarious basis can have lasting effects for good or bad on others with whom we associate.

A very interesting experiment was done many years ago by Dr. Emanuel Cheraskin, a much respected nutritional colleague. He was teaching a class of embryonic physicians and wanted to emphasize how relative values can be mistaken for fact. He posed several questions to each student regarding what they thought was normal weight, height, blood pressure, cholesterol, etc. After the exam was over, he correlated each of their answers with their personal characteristics and found that the fat doctors gave a much higher weight for normalcy, the tall doctors gave a much taller height for normalcy, and the doctors with higher blood pressure or higher cholesterol thought that higher values were normal. It was interesting to note that most of the answers were relative to their own personal characteristics. So keep in mind that all of our beliefs are colored by our personal education, experience, and lifestyle; and none of us has all the answers, as hard as we may try.

I feel that I am an extremely fortunate person in so many ways. I have a loving family of whom I am very proud. I have been able to attain a very satisfactory level of health, and I enjoy helping people to try to do the same. It is easy to be happy when it is a joy to go to work. One reason I like my work is because I have so many very nice patients. I love to see my patients get better and enjoy life. It is a great satisfaction to know that I have been useful.

16

Attention Deficit Disorder: A Parent's Nightmare

It is an unfortunate circumstance that in a land of plenty, so many of our children are being raised malnourished—often because of the foods and nutritional instructions ordered by their doctors. The doctors are not necessarily to be condemned since, with rare exceptions, they receive all of their nutritional information from various food manufacturers. It is a rare circumstance to acquire any good nutritional information in medical school since such classes rarely exist. We doctors get most of our information on nutrition from food company advertising or in medical journals which are replete with "factual studies" financed by grants from food companies. Unfortunately for the public, the results of these studies are too often influenced by the "bottom line," which is the profit motive. Hence, we are subject to the same influences that you are, and we wind up with the same faulty "knowledge" of fats, sugars, diet foods, artificial sweeteners, and vitamins and minerals that you do.

Because there isn't enough good information available on child nutrition, we raise them on "foods" (that are many times not foods at all), which have devastating effects on the child's physical and mental health. Below is the story of such a sad result of improper nutrition resulting in the frequent physical illness and increasing mental disability of this young patient. In this case, the experts called it Attention Deficit Disorder.

On September 30, 1991, a fourteen-year-old girl—we'll call her Ann—came into my office accompanied by her mother. I had previously talked to the mother on the phone and gotten a rather detailed history of Ann's problems. I had also received her complete medical file since age two from the doctors who had cared for her.

From the time she was a baby, Ann had frequently been sick with sore throats, upper respiratory infections, stomach aches, and allergies. These had always been treated with antibiotics and antihistamines. At age six, she had mononucleosis and subsequent pneumonia for which she had taken lots of antibiotics. When she was eight years old, she started having problems at school. She became very slow in doing her work. She didn't get her homework done. Her attention span became very short, and she was constantly causing problems in the classroom. Her grades began to deteriorate so that she was getting D's and incompletes instead of her usual A's and B's.

A series of visits to doctor's offices culminated in the diagnosis of Attention Deficit Disorder, and she was placed on Ritalin (10 mg. per day). For a few weeks, she became much more alert and cooperative, and her grades improved only to have her condition gradually deteriorate again. For the next several years, the dose of Ritalin was gradually increased until she was taking a total of 40 mg. per day. When she was twelve years old, she began to develop acne and was put on constant antibiotic therapy for the next two years with questionable success.

On her first visit to my office, she was having a lot of mental confusion when she tried to do her school work. Her attention span was very short. She was causing problems in the classroom. She was depressed, constantly fatigued, and gaining excessive weight.

Analysis of her diet revealed a large intake of refined flour foods, sugared drinks, and milk. She ate some meat and cooked vegetables but no fresh food, and she took no vitamin or mineral supplements. She was taking prescriptions for Ritalin and Tetracycline.

My examination revealed a somewhat shy fourteen-year-old girl with nonremarkable findings except for a moderate case of acne on the nose and cheeks and about 15 lbs. of extra weight.

I went along with the previous diagnosis of ADD but added another diagnosis of chronic systemic candidiasis. This second diagnosis should probably have been the primary diagnosis all the time except that orthodox physicians don't generally recognize it as a problem.

Ann's treatment consisted of a very nutritious diet which eliminated all of the refined flour and sugar foods as well as cheese and milk. This, of course, stopped her sugared drink intake also. I put her on a moderate strength vitamin and mineral tablet, 200 mg. of B6, 25,000 units of natural vitamin A, 1,500 mg. of niacinamide, 2,000 mg. of vitamin C, and 100 mg. of zinc daily. I told the mother to reduce the Ritalin to 20 mg. a day for one week and then continue to reduce it by 5 mg. a week until she was no longer taking it. I also prescribed one fourth of a teaspoon of Nystatin powder twice daily. Since they lived in a town about 100 miles away from my office, I told the mother to call me in two weeks and to bring Ann back in six weeks.

In two weeks, the mother called to tell me that Ann was doing "great." The ADD was much improved, and the depression and mental confusion were gone. Her skin was clearing, and her energy was much better.

Ann returned to my office one month after the phone call. She looked like a different girl. Her facial expression was alive. The acne was about 80 percent gone. She had no more depression or mental confusion and was getting A's and B's in school again. Her mother also reported that she was off Ritalin, and her self-confidence was much improved. She had also lost 9 lbs. I reduced all of her vitamin doses to about half and dismissed her from care.

This was admittedly a very rapid recovery for a patient who had been having some serious problems for such a long period of time. Not all patients respond this rapidly, but almost all respond. I believe much of the rapid success in this case can be attributed to Ann. This young patient realized she had a very definite problem that was adversely affecting her life and the lives of those around her, and she cooperated with the treatment 100 percent.

Patient cooperation isn't always this good. However, it does emphasize the fact that the recuperative power of nature can be great indeed, and sometimes it can create what almost seems to be a miracle—at least in the eyes of distraught parents.

I have seen many patients with ADD. Almost all of them also have either hypoglycemia or chronic systemic candidiasis or both. In my opinion, most of these learning and attention disorders are merely symptoms of a much deeper underlying problem. Once the underlying problem is corrected, the so-called "brain disorder" goes away. This condition used to be called hyperactivity, but I suspect that name didn't command the awe that Attention Deficit Disorder does. Dyslexia is closely related to this same problem. All are disturbances of normal brain function due to altered brain chemistry.

Last night I was sitting on the deck of my mountain home observing the brilliance of the thousands of stars in an otherwise clear sky. They seemed so close as to be almost within my grasp. It was August 11th, and I had read that on this night, an abundance of falling stars and meteors would be visible in the skies. I was not disappointed. While I reclined and thrilled at the small part of the universe which is visible to us, dozens of stars seemed to literally fall out of the sky only to disappear after an extended, rapid journey into who knows where? On three different occasions, a large ball of fire swept halfway across the sky with a long tail of light trailing after it, again to disappear into who knows where? If I had been home, the magnificence of this scene probably would have been much less spectacular because of the lower altitude and the lights of civilization. Yet, the beauty still would have been there whether I saw it or not.

The celestial bodies which make up the universe are so vast and wonderful that we will never be able to fully understand their origin or their purpose. It occurred to me while I was meditating, that the stars I was watching are made of matter. They have no ability to feel or see or communicate with one another. It then struck me that while the beauty I was observing was something very special, it couldn't begin to compare to how special we are as human beings.

We are made up not only of matter, but we have been made in the image of God. We have the ability to think and reason, and we have a conscience to define right from wrong. We have the capacity to feel and to love and to help others share their joys. The belief that we are very special has a great influence on our physical health. Some of you may have lost confidence in yourselves or possibly never had it. No matter what the circumstances, the fact remains that you are a very special person.

The mind is a sponge that soaks up everything that it hears. Many people are handicapped from childhood because they have been led to believe (or have been told outright) that they are no good or not worthy. They then grow up with the false subconscious feeling that they are not deserving of love or happiness. These negative feelings are converted by the body into harmful chemistry that is certainly capable of helping to destroy an otherwise healthy body.

Fortunately, the mind also has the power to change those harmful subconscious feelings. So many symptoms can be partially eliminated by appreciation of the fact that you are a very special person—one of a kind. There will never be another person on this earth who looks the same, feels the same, or has the same capacity to influence other people. Just the true realization that you are so special should create in you the positive environment that is so essential to good health.

So much of the juvenile and gang-related crime is directly the result of children who have never had the opportunity to know that they are very special people. People who know that they are very special in the eyes of those who nurtured them don't need to find that satisfaction in a negative way by joining gangs. I feel very sorry for human beings who are raised where beauty of any kind is a forgotten quality. I feel sorry for children who are raised in cities where they rarely, if ever, get to experience the beauty of grass and trees and the clear sky unimpeded by smoke and smog. I feel sorry for children who grow up in homes where hugging and expressions of love are considered an unnecessary or unmanly waste of time. I feel sorry for parents and adults who rarely, if ever, hug their children. I feel sorry for adults who have ruined their own lives and their children's lives because they never learned that tenderness and expressions of love are strong qualities and not signs of weakness. I feel extremely sorry for all people who rarely or never experience the feeling of warmth and closeness that a hug or expression of love can bring.

I don't ever want you to forget that regardless of the fact that there may be some disharmony or ugliness in your life, you a very special person, and just that belief can make you happier and healthier.

17

Reactive Hypoglycemia

A significant percentage of the population suffers from a devastating illness that brings heartache and depression. Most of the medical profession doesn't even recognize it as a medical problem. The condition is reactive hypoglycemia.

The brain is the master switchboard which controls the functions of the human body. The energy it utilizes comes primarily from the simple sugar—glucose. In a normal functioning body, the glucose level of the blood stays within relatively steady boundaries—between 70 mg.% and 110 mg.%. That means that there are about 70 to 110 mg. of glucose (what you think of as sugar) for every 100 milliliters (about 1/3 of a cup) of blood in your body. As long as the sugar level remains constant, the brain functions normally, and all is well. The sugar that is derived from good, wholesome food is released into the blood stream very slowly. Hence, only small amounts of insulin (the hormone that helps control the blood sugar level) is required of the pancreas.

The ingestion of large amounts of refined sugar and refined flour (which is converted rapidly into sugar) causes a very rapid increase in the blood sugar level since little or no digestion is necessary. The blood sugar rises to much higher levels than normal, and the body's protective mechanism declares an emergency. Thus, the pancreas begins to produce much higher amounts of insulin than usual to bring the blood sugar back to its normal level.

However, after many years of this kind of abuse, the control mechanism begins to malfunction and the pancreas produces too much insulin in these emergency situations. As a consequence, the blood sugar is driven to levels too low for proper operation of the brain. Remember, the brain runs on glucose. Another emergency situation has now arisen, and in order to keep the blood sugar from reaching dangerously low levels, the adrenal glands begin to produce more adrenaline than is normal in order to stimulate the liver to release some of its stored sugar in an effort to get the blood sugar back to normal. Nature also causes the patient to crave something sweet for the same reason. Adrenaline, however, is the hormone that makes the body get ready for fight or flight. So, it causes the heart to race and the nervous system to over-stimulate. The end result is a patient with a myriad of symptoms ranging from fatigue, depression, and poor brain ability to tachycardia (rapid heart beat), hyperactivity, crying spells, and a feeling of fear of impending disaster, depending on which cycle of the malfunction the patient is in.

This condition generally takes years of nutritional abuse before the sugar control mechanism breaks down sufficiently to produce the above mentioned problems. Vitamin and mineral deficiencies develop over a period of time due to the ingestion of so much sugar and refined food. It requires a lot of vitamin B complex, zinc, magnesium, chromium, and other nutrients to metabolize sugar. Since there are no vitamins and minerals in sugar, the body steals from the reserves in its body tissues to supply these necessary ingredients, and the body reserves finally are depleted. Then, deficiency symptoms begin to appear.

This is a disease of civilization brought on by the tremendous overuse of sugar and white flour products such as soft drinks (regular or diet—it makes no difference), cakes, pies, cookies, ice cream, and refined breads. How foolish we are to think that our bodies can exist healthfully on junk foods that cannot supply the necessary vitamins and minerals required for proper body chemistry. Even more ludicrous is the fact that much of the medical profession does not even recognize the problem.

A significant percentage of the U.S. population live much of their lives with fatigue, depression, crying spells, inability to think properly, muscle problems, joint aches, fluid retention, menstrual problems, tachycardia, and myriads of other symptoms. They may have spent thousands of dollars for diagnostic workups by all sorts of specialists only to be told that it is essentially "all in your head" or that it's stress and you must "get hold of yourself." Or finally, they may have been told that they need to see a psychiatrist. What a shame!

About three years ago, a very distraught husband came to my office with a sad and frightening story, asking for my help. He said his wife, about fifty years of age, had been very energetic and vivacious until she had a major surgery about a year before. Since that time, she had begun to experience symptoms of fatigue and insecurity for which she consulted her doctor who found nothing abnormal in the laboratory tests. The symptoms became gradually more severe, and she was referred to other physicians who performed more and more diagnostic workups. The tests produced no answers. Her depression became so severe that she became like a zombie, having hallucinations and becoming incapable of taking care of herself. She was put in the psychiatric ward of a hospital and after the use of many drugs, which brought no improvement, the husband was told that she would have to be committed to the state mental hospital. He had an appointment there the following week.

I agreed to try to help and requested copies of all the laboratory work which had been done on her the past year. Every finding was negative *except* the six-hour glucose tolerance test, which showed a highly fluctuating blood sugar that dropped at the fifth hour to 50 mg.%! This finding had been completely neglected as insignificant. I immediately started this patient on a wholesome diet, completely sugar-free. I prescribed frequent feedings and large doses of all the vitamins and minerals both by mouth and by I.V. injection. Many years ago, I learned from Dr. Abram Hoffer, an orthomolecular psychiatrist, the importance of the B vitamins, especially niacinamide, in the treatment of so-called "mental disorders." I have used niacinamide with such success in cases like this that I have dubbed it "nature's antidepressant."

In this particular case, the patient was given oral daily divided doses of 100 mg. of B complex and 3,000 mg. of niacinamide. Judicious supplementation with other nutrients also was used. To make a long story short, within a week the patient was lucid again and was able to smile a little. Within a month, she was off all the drugs and was regaining her energy and performing most of her normal duties. At the end of about three months, she was completely well and back to her energetic and vivacious self. I rarely see her as a patient anymore, but she drops by quite frequently just to say hello and to express her gratitude. The diagnosis wasn't insanity—only reactive hypoglycemia.

I want to share with you a very wonderful surprise our children had in store for my wife and me for our 50th wedding anniversary. Our oldest daughter, Karen, had been commissioned to put together a book made up of pictures, letters, memoirs, anniversary cards, etc., from family, relatives, friends, and patients. The book depicts memorable events in our lives from the time we were going together as sweethearts until the present time.

The three-inch thick book is entitled "It's A Wonderful Life." And so it has been. The book was presented to us when Karen and her family came to Lubbock to visit. Some of the pictures brought back so many memories—many of them events which had slipped from my mind. So many letters and cards from my patients expressing in a very touching way how their health had been changed and their lives enriched because of the help that I had been privileged to render. There were so many letters from relatives recounting happy times that have made life such a blessing.

Some of the most touching recollections came from our children, grandchildren, and nieces who related instances of things we had done with them in the past which had made such a deep impression on them and their lives. Events that they still remembered but had long ago slipped from our memories.

I must admit that as I spent the two or three hours that it took to review the entire book, I seldom had a dry eye. It impressed on me in a very emphatic manner something of which we all should be constantly aware: each of our lives touch so many other lives in ways that we may never know, and we should be very careful to make sure that those influences are for good.

18

Panic Attacks

I feel very strongly about wanting to help my patients with their various disabilities. Some conditions are quite chronic, and while they are nonetheless important to the patient and to me, the urgency of assistance is nowhere more demanding than in the treatment of panic attack disorders.

Many people have some person either in their family or among their intimate acquaintances who suffers with panic attacks. Victims of this puzzling malady are capable of hiding it from their friends and relatives for a period of time—maybe several months or years—while only the husband or wife or immediate family are aware of the devastating changes taking place in the life and behavior of their loved one.

The problem arises very slowly at first, manifest only by the patient noticing some increasing fatigue that wasn't present a month or two before. As the fatigue increases, the patient notices a lack of interest in social events that were at one time very enjoyable. Depression begins to rear its ugly head, and as time passes, becomes more and more severe. If the patient is lucky enough to get proper and adequate help at this point, the problem may never advance to the next stage—the stage which makes this patient seek immediate assistance of some kind. Frequently, during a period of sleeplessness, (which is a common problem in these cases) the patient will experience a sudden and frightful spell of very rapid heart beat and the sensation of breathlessness and fear of impending disaster. The patient is often rushed to the emergency room of a local hospital where he or she is run through all kinds of laboratory tests and expensive diagnostic work only to be told that he or she is "stressed out" and given a sedative of some kind. These spells continue with increasing frequency until the patient finally lands in the psychiatric ward of a hospital to be treated with various mind-altering drugs. These drugs may alleviate some of the symptoms but are not without unpleasant, and many times serious, side effects. Believe me, the solution to this problem is not to be found in drug treatment.

If you have never known a person with panic attack disorder or have never had this disorder yourself, it would be difficult for you to appreciate the complete devastation it can cause to a life or a family. After repeated failing attempts to find satisfactory medical help, the thought of living under these conditions loses its appeal, and serious consequences can result. I must admit that I have had many sleepless nights while treating patients in the advanced stage of this disorder.

This is what most doctors think of as a "psychiatric" condition. While it definitely alters normal brain function, the basic cause of the abnormality is biochemical and has to be treated as such if satisfactory and permanent results are to be obtained. In my opinion and experience, these patients have malfunctioning glucose metabolism—a reactive type of hypoglycemia—which must be corrected if the patient is to become well and happy again.

The complete treatment of this very complicated condition cannot be outlined in "cook book" fashion without having personal contact with the patient and knowing some of the details of his or her lifestyle. I am, however, going to outline the basic things that I find necessary in treating most panic attack disorders.

First, this is a problem that I find present in many more women than men—probably eight or ten to one. The reason for this plurality in women is not positively identifiable, but I suspect that the differences in hormone makeup have a lot to do with it.

All the patients I have seen with panic attacks have a diet that is sadly deficient in the necessary chemicals that operate the brain. Since the brain is the electrical switchboard of the body, these deficiencies make many of the control mechanisms of the body go "haywire." Thus, the many symptoms of panic attack occur. The eating and drinking habits of these patients are extremely important. Without exception, these patients eat far too many refined sugar and white flour foods, and this must be stopped. Soft drinks (diet or regular, it makes no difference) are often major offenders. The patient must begin to eat ample supplies of *raw* fruits and vegetables and *whole grain* breads and cereals. Intake of good protein foods such as eggs, beans, nuts, and moderate amounts of good meats are also necessary.

Certain deficiencies in vitamins and minerals are *always* found in panic attack patients. These deficiencies have been coming on for a long time, but until they become severe enough, the body can "make do." But after a certain point, the body can no longer cope and the symptoms begin. The B vitamins are always necessary as is the all important mineral, magnesium. These supplements are given by oral ingestion and by intravenous injection. These are not the only ones, but they are critical to the treatment. Usually, much larger doses than the RDA (which is far too little to start with) are given.

With strict adherence to the above treatment and correction of any other obvious detrimental lifestyle habits, such as smoking or excessive intake of coffee and/or alcohol, these patients generally can be returned to a useful and happy life in only a few months. One of my greatest satisfactions in this business is seeing someone who comes to me in utter despair become a happy, smiling, productive person, again enjoying life. The sleepless nights are worth it.

I lost a good friend last month. It's a sad thing to lose a friend. I suppose I should try to learn to get accustomed to it. After all, as we get older, all of our friends are getting older too. I understand that, and I know that this life is not eternal, but I hate the thought of leaving those I love. Until a few months before his death, my friend did too. He had been through an awful lot of hardship and stress the last two years of his life. His wife had died just a year before after going through months of surgeries and medical treatments to no avail. I think it was just as hard on him as it was on her—the seemingly endless trips to M.D. Anderson Hospital in Houston and to hospitals here in town. They were a devoted couple that Lynne and I had known for thirty-five years.

About two weeks before his wife died, my friend discovered that he had cancer. He was just seventy years old. He had lived a very full and productive life. He had suffered much as a prisoner of war during World War II. He was a local television newscaster for many years in Lubbock. He contributed his talents unselfishly to many civic endeavors and charity boards. He was a man who had strong beliefs and wasn't afraid to stand by his convictions. I admired him for that.

He is survived by two wonderful children, whom he loved dearly. They are outstanding examples of young people. He also had five grandchildren for whom he had a soft spot in his heart. He was a man who at times might have seemed to have a rough exterior, but all who knew him saw his tender heart.

There was a time or two during his year-long fight for life that it seemed he might whip his illness. During those weeks, I could see the joy in his heart. However, as the weeks and months passed, it became painfully evident that the treatment was failing and he became resigned to death. I think the last two or three weeks of his life he actually welcomed death.

During those last couple of months when he was pretty much house bound, I visited him quite frequently, as did several of his other friends. When a person realizes he is going to die shortly, the true person emerges, devoid of all window dressing. We talked about many of his accomplishments and experiences in life. We talked about his wonderful family and the pride they gave him. We talked many times about death and the beginning of a new life. He had a strong belief in God. He was not afraid to die. He expressed that to me many times.

It is a male trait, I suppose, to have difficulty expressing tenderness or affection, but when the chips are down and death is impending, many learned barriers are cast aside. He said many things in the last few days of his life that I shall never forget, but the thing that touched me the most he said just two days before he died. He was very weak and had difficulty staying on his feet, but as I left that night he insisted on seeing me to the door. As I reached the door I put my arm on his shoulder and he said: "I sure do love you guys." I'm glad I am writing this because there is no way my emotions would let me relate it otherwise.

I was a pallbearer at his family grave side service, and his friends and family gave many testimonials. But, his worth as a man was expressed most eloquently by one of his little grandsons who said with tears in his voice: "He was a great grandad."

It's strange, isn't it, how each man's life touches so many others, and when he's not around it leaves an awful hole. My friend touched the lives of untold numbers of people, and his passing has indeed left an awful hole. If you get nothing else from what I write, please remember how precious your life is.

19

Premenstrual Syndrome (PMS)

At least 75 percent of my patients are women. I don't know exactly what the reason for this is, but I suspect it has a lot to do with the fact that women are much less stubborn than men and give in more quickly to seeking help for their ailments. It also may have to do with the fact that because of the difference in hormone make-up, many of the health problems that I see are found more often in women. Be that as it may, this lesson in health is specifically addressed to women but is a subject in which men have a very definite interest also, especially when "that time" rolls around.

Many of the problems between husband and wife and wife and family are caused by premenstrual syndrome, which can be extremely devastating to some women (and generally, needlessly so). It can be not only a very serious family problem, but it is a very serious social problem as well. It is a statistical fact that most crimes committed by women—murder, robbery, child abuse, suicide—are committed during the premenstrual phase.

Like most other health problems, the medical profession has made PMS a very complicated problem, which requires detailed laboratory work up and complicated drug supervision. My years of experience with the successful treatment of this condition has indicated otherwise. PMS is *not* a disease. Like most other medical conditions, it has been given an awe inspiring medical name but generally responds quite well to simple solutions. It is merely a group of symptoms, usually caused by inadequacies in lifestyle. These inadequacies are usually nutritional and are easily correctable if the patient has the desire to overcome her problems.

With proper treatment, improvement of symptoms usually can be seen with the second menstrual period and many times completely eliminated within three to six months. The accepted medical treatment for this problem is usually the administration of hormones, diuretics, and antidepressants, which many times make the patient feel worse from the side effects of the drugs. At best, it merely covers up the cause of the symptoms.

Before I explain how to overcome this problem, I want you to understand a little bit about what I believe to be the cause. This is not orthodox medical opinion. Over the years, I have become aware of the fact that almost all women with PMS have significant amounts of fluid retention starting most remarkably about the same time as the irritability, weight gain, puffiness, breast tenderness, depression, and anxiety. Fluid retention is not only present in the visible parts of the body but also in the brain, which severely affects the neurotransmitting system. This in turn accounts for the drastic changes in personality and thinking during this phase of the monthly cycle.

The answer would then seem to be quite obvious and would certainly concur with medical thinking—give the patient a diuretic to induce excess urination and get rid of the excess fluid. Oops, the answer is not quite that simple. Diuretic drugs not only rid the body of excess fluids but also cause the loss of potassium, magnesium, B complex, B6, and some other vitamins and minerals that are necessary to the brain's neurotransmitting system. There is a much better answer.

The basic cause of fluid accumulation is caused by the ingestion of refined carbohydrates—principally refined flour and sugar. Most of the women I treat who have significant PMS have big cravings for sweets and drink considerable amounts of soft drinks. Most also have definite clinical deficiencies of the B complex vitamins and particularly vitamin B6. Magnesium is also generally lacking. The effective treatment is then quite simple. Stop the ingestion of refined carbohydrates (including all soft drinks). In my estimation, soft drinks are among the most injurious products to our general health.

In addition to eliminating the harmful foods from the diet, a conscientious effort must be made to include plenty of fiber and vitamin rich foods. Vitamin and mineral supplements are also very important. Doses vary according to individual need, but generally speaking should include about 50 mg. of B complex, 100 mg. of B6, 300 to 600 mg. of magnesium, and 400 to 800 units of vitamin E.

I have seen families saved and lives changed by employing these simple but common sense suggestions. However, anyone who is being treated for this problem should certainly not cease present treatment without adequate supervision by a nutritionally oriented physician.

There are so many things that I want my patients to know. I see so many people who are suffering because of the neglect of simple truths that I have learned over the years. I am equally sure that I have endured many trials in my life from which I could have been spared if only someone had been able to impart to me some piece of valuable knowledge from their experience. That assumes that I would have been receptive to learning and that is where the catch comes in. So many times I see patients who have problems that I know I could help if only I could find a way to make them want to believe. The old adage was never more true: "You can lead a horse to water, but you can't make him drink."

In most cases, health is such a simple thing. There is no mysterious secret that only those who have studied disease for years can give you. The time to start thinking about being well and feeling well is before devastating disease processes have taken their toll. The less degeneration that has taken place, the quicker and easier the process of recovery. There are few instances where disease will continue to exist if the patient has the desire, intestinal fortitude, and patience to make the simple and necessary changes in lifestyle to accomplish the desired goal. This should be the doctor's role—to be the guide to optimal health, not only a diagnostician of disease. The same things that can keep us healthy can also get us healthy!

It is an ironic truth that we begin to die from the moment we are born! Few of us ever think about birth in this fashion, and I'm sure it is more pleasant not to do so, but the fact remains. The degenerative process begins with the first breath. If the newborn is fortunate enough to have parents who are somewhat informed or anxious to learn some of the simple rules of health, he or she will mature with far fewer of the common ailments of the young and have a better chance of escaping the devastating diseases of the old. It should be the duty and the burning desire of the doctor to accomplish this goal. Degeneration of the human body is an inescapable truth that we cannot stop. With careful attention to our living habits and respect for our bodies, however, we can at least slow the process and keep it from wreaking havoc on us as we age as gracefully as possible.

20

Breast Cancer

There are few words that strike fear and panic in the minds and hearts of women and their families more than the two words "breast cancer." You are being told that 1 of every 8 women will be victims of this dread disease, and then you are advised on the many expensive, inconvenient, and worrisome things you must do to try to protect yourselves. You are led to believe that 1 out of 8 women you meet walking down the street or waiting in your doctor's waiting room either have or will have cancer of the breast at their present age. Nonsense! Statistics can be very misleading unless all the facts are known and properly presented. Statistics are to some of these people what a lamppost is to a drunk—more for support than for illumination.

You have to remember that the most important risk factor for developing breast cancer is age. According to a recent issue of *Family Practice News*, if you are a thirty-year-old white woman in this country, your chance of developing breast cancer is 1 in 5,900! Yes, you read it right. That sounds better than 1 in 8, wouldn't you say?

If you are a fifty-year-old woman, your chance of developing breast cancer is about 1 in 590; at sixty, 1 in 420; at seventy, 1 in 330; and at ninety-five years of age (*if* you live that long) your risk is 1 in 10. In other words, what you have been beaten over the head with in all the news reports really is that if you live to be ninety-five, you have a 1 in 10 chance of developing breast cancer.

Now let's carry the truth about these statistics a little farther. The numbers I have just quoted are only for the possibility of *developing* breast cancer, not dying from it. If you live to be ninety-five and are one of the ten who will develop breast cancer, there is only a 1 in 28 chance that you will die from it! You will probably die from old age long before dying of cancer, and that is something we can't do much about.

These differences would also apply to the younger age groups. Also keep in mind that these figures apply to the general population who have atrocious diets and living habits! The statistics for those of you who are conscious of the needs of your body would be *much more* favorable than that since there are many things that can be done to prevent cancer.

Please don't misunderstand. I do not belittle the gravity of breast cancer. To the person who develops it, the statistics are 100 percent. The current medical thinking is that the billions of dollars that are spent in frequent cancer exams and mammograms are worth it if only the life of one person can be saved. This is very magnanimous thinking, but what if some of the numerous routine things we do to detect early breast cancers may be causing some of the cancers that develop later?

Thorough studies from other countries reveal that women under the age of fifty who have routine annual mammograms have more breast cancer after age fifty than the general population. The organized medical community in this country does not accept those findings. However, even in this country, there is more and more controversy about the wisdom of routine mammograms in younger women.

I certainly don't want you to even start to believe that I have the answer to this problem. I do know that the radiation experienced in a single mammogram is very small. However, I do not know what the accumulative effect of repeated radiation will be, and I don't think anyone else does. If there was an absolutely *right* answer, there wouldn't be any controversy about it.

Mammography is a big advance in the diagnosis of cancer of the breast. That, we can say with certainty. We can also say that different radiologists sometimes interpret mammograms quite differently and that there are many unnecessary breast biopsies done because of this. I think mammograms are wonderful diagnostic tools, but I believe they should be tempered by knowledge of the patient, family history, and physical examination.

I can almost read your mind! You are thinking, "what about fibrocystic breast disease (FBD) and things I can do to *prevent* these dreaded problems?" FBD is an accumulation of abnormal cystic tissue in the fatty tissue of the breast. Many times the patient or doctor can feel it during an examination. Mammograms and ultrasound examination can generally differentiate between FBD and cancer. According to the Family Practice News report, women who have FBD *and* one first degree relative with breast cancer have about a nine times increased risk of developing breast cancer. If you don't have both conditions existing, your chances are about the same as any other woman.

It is thought that FBD is stimulated by the ingestion of xanthenes, which include coffee, tea, chocolate, soft drinks, and other caffeine containing foods and drinks. In my experience, FBD is also stimulated by the intake of sugar. Generally speaking, cysts in the breast can be reduced very satisfactorily by conscientious changes in diet and intake of adequate amounts of certain vitamins and minerals.

Preventing breast problems is by far more desirable than treating them once they have occurred! If we would only spend one-tenth the money on nutritional research that we spend on the spectacular methods of diagnosis and treatment, breast cancer could be more of a rarity than an expected event. However, preventing the problem is not nearly as profitable as treating it, and the bottom line frequently calls the shots.

Preventing some of these breast problems is of course not a 100 percent possibility. Heredity and genetics are very important, but we should have a much better record of prevention than we do. Much is known about the nutritional prevention of breast problems. Conventional medical wisdom, however, has very little interest in it. I have said in previous chapters that the same things that get a body healthy, keep a body healthy. The breast is merely part of the body, and it is impossible to have a diseased breast and a healthy body. In some cases, it just happens to be the place where the body happens to evidence the ravages of disease.

There are many things you can do to reduce or eliminate your chances of ever having breast cancer. Some of the important "do's" and "don'ts" are as follows:

1. Eliminate the use of refined foods as nearly as possible.

2. Eliminate the use of sugar products.
3. Eliminate the use of white flour products.
4. Do not use partially hydrogenated fat products such as margarine and the altered foods termed "low fat" and "diet."
5. Eat large quantities of raw foods such as vegetables, fruits, nuts, and whole grain cereals and bread products.
6. Reduce your intake of red meats.
7. Drink plenty of pure water (not chlorinated).
8. Get lots of exercise.
9. Cultivate complete and regular bowel movements. If you are constipated, you may need to supplement your diet with extra fiber, such as raw bran flakes.
10. Correct any indigestion problems with pancreatic enzymes. They can be found at health food stores.
11. Ensure a generous intake of antioxidants like vitamin C, vitamin A (and its precursor, beta carotene), vitamin E complex, selenium, and zinc.
12. Ensure adequate amounts of some of the other minerals like magnesium, calcium, and chromium.
13. Don't smoke.

It is impossible to name all of the things that any given individual needs because each person needs different things and different quantities, but the above is a good general rundown. The vitamins and minerals are generally needed in much greater quantities than the RDA stipulates.

Well, I hope I have been able to shed enough light on this subject to reduce some of the fears that you may have had. I know that some of my patients have been very concerned. If I have been able to give you information that will help you to sleep better at night, and if I have been able to show you to some extent how the statistical system is sometimes twisted, I have been well paid. Just don't believe everything you hear on television or read in the papers. Sometimes it's just not so.

Tonight as I sit in my usual spot on the deck of my Alto home, I see a scene that I have seen many times. Tonight, however, it seems to have a special significance. It seems that a finite amount of sky is outlined by the vertical posts that support the vaulted roof of the deck. In that finite view is a scene that would be a challenge to the brush of an artist such as Windberg. A brilliant half-moon is visible in the center of the framed area with the brilliance of Venus just below and to the left of the moon. Part of the Big Dipper is to the right. For some reason, tonight the moon seems to be much closer to my deck, and it seems to be shining just for me at this moment as if to tell me to stop the passage of time and count the blessings I have been given. And for the next few minutes, I tried to do just that.

As I was thinking, it occurred to me how much our lives are the culmination of our choices. In this country, we are so blessed with the freedom to choose. However, it also occurred to me how that freedom can also be a curse. In our early teenage years when we begin to assume some personal control over our lives, the opportunities to make new and unsupervised decisions abound. If we have been fortunate enough to have had some concerned guidance in our early years, we may have developed enough wisdom and experience to make good choices regarding the friends we choose, the activities we pursue, the attitudes we form, and the myriads of ever-present temptations with which teenagers have to contend. As we get older, we receive either a blessing or a curse from those choices. If the choices have been very bad, we may have the potential for ruining the rest of our lives. If good, or at least not too bad, we get the chance to stay in the game and make additional choices with the aid of more experience under our belts. We may not be fully aware at the time we make choices that those choices will influence not only our own lives but also the lives of untold numbers of people within the sphere of our influence.

Do you think that there is only so much health around and that every person is given just a certain amount that will have to last him or her until death? Of course not! If your health is not predetermined, the only other conclusion is that it can be influenced by your choices. In that event, it follows that you have a good deal of control over your health according to the choices you make. If you are aware that "junk foods" such as sugar, refined flour, and partially hydrogenated fats are detrimental to your health and you choose to eat them, those are bad decisions, and you will surely suffer for them. If you refrain from eating that kind of food, your body will thank you, and you will benefit from it with a healthier, longer, and more enjoyable life.

Without belaboring the point, the same holds true for all the other bad choices we make for our bodies. To bring this thought to the conclusion that I pointed out in the previous paragraph, when we make bad choices in relation to our health, we may think that we are only hurting ourselves and that it should be our right to choose—and so it may be from a selfish point of view. However, stop to think of some other consequences of those poor decisions. A poor state of health will throw a heavy burden on those you love, not only from the possible financial burden, but also from the psycho-logical stress involved. An early death may leave your family without the strength and guidance of a mother or father or without the assets to care for them—because of poor choices. To carry this analogy a little further, you only have to stop and think a moment to realize the financial burden that you are carrying right now to pay for the sustenance and so called "health care" of a significant percentage of our population because of the poor choices they have made throughout their lives. Think about it. Wouldn't it be wise to make the simple choices now to insure your good health and that of your loved ones?

21

Chronic Systemic Candidiasis

Until about fifteen years ago, I could not have enlightened you on this very vital subject. At that time, I didn't know that it existed. I was seeing many patients with its chronic, devastating manifestations, but I was not recognizing the problem for what it was. I was privileged about that time to attend a convention in Atlanta, Georgia, sponsored by the Huxley Institute for Biosocial Research. This is an organization whose purpose is advancing nutritional research. The Huxley Institute also holds seminars to train open-minded professionals in the health field about alternative methods of treating various puzzling and debilitating diseases.

Orian Truss, M.D., was one of the lecturers—a man who opened my eyes to a serious condition which is still largely unrecognized by the medical profession. That condition is chronic systemic candidiasis. It is not only ignored, but it is actually being caused by the overuse of many drugs—particularly antibiotics. Because of the knowledge I gained from Dr. Truss and my subsequent study of the problem, I have been privileged to assist hundreds of patients to regain a status of health that has made their lives worth living again.

First, let me tell you about the problem. Candida is a type of yeast. Candida is one of the most primitive of organisms, and is everywhere in nature. There is no way to escape contact with it since it is present in the air, on the food we eat, and on the surfaces of the furniture in our homes. Generally, this yeast (Candida Albicans) is quite harmless to humans because the body was designed with an automatic protective mechanism—the immune system. Although we constantly breathe, eat, and contact candida organisms, they do us no harm *if* the immune system is working up to par. The normal bacteria in our intestinal tract, acidophilus, prevents the overgrowth of candida.

Acidophilus thrive in the normal habitat of the bowel and under conditions that nature intended. The normal bacteria (acidophilus) in the bowel have many definite functions including digestion of food, manufacture of vitamin B, and policemen preventing the over-growth of yeast. Powerful antibiotics and drugs kill the normal bacteria in the bowel. The end result of the frequent or continued use of antibiotics and almost all painkilling drugs is sterilization of the bowel. As a result, the yeast overgrow and invade the body. With the development and promotion of the new and broad spectrum antibiotics by pharmaceutical companies and their injudicious use by doctors, the unrecognized disease—systemic candidiasis—is becoming more and more common and ruining more and more lives.

Antibiotics are wonderful, and at times, life-saving drugs. But, it is the almost universal *overuse* of these drugs that is leaving us exposed to more and more bacteria which have become immune to antibiotics. Although many bacteria are becoming immune to antibiotics, the drugs still have the capacity to kill the acidophilus your body needs for the enhancement of your immune system. The end result is the development of strains of bacteria which cause diseases against which antibiotics are totally ineffective. At the same time, the immune system becomes suppressed to the point where it is incapable of protecting the body against yeast. Hence, we may not only have no protection from the antibiotic, but we have lessened protection from the body's own protective mechanism. The development of systemic candidiasis can cause a myriad of puzzling symptoms which can make living a miserable experience.

If you have watched any of the medical advice programs on television lately, you have probably heard about the development of new strains of bacteria which have become resistant to antibiotics. The medical community fears that diseases will develop for which there is no effective medical treatment. How true! We are seeing it every day. The sad part is that not only can the medical treatment become ineffective, but it actually causes the systemic candida problem. This creates a "double whammy" since the immune system has been damaged and cannot do the protective job for which it was designed. As a result, the poor patient suffers unnecessarily.

Think with me for a minute. Your child gets a cold or an ear infection and you take him to the doctor. The doctor has to do something that you can't do yourself or you would think he isn't worth what you are paying him. So, many times the doctor prescribes antibiotics even though he may feel that they are not really necessary. Sometimes antibiotics are very necessary but not nearly as often as they are used. The public has been so brainwashed by the pharmaceutical industry and the medical associations into believing that we can't get well without doctors and drugs that we are spending billions of dollars making ourselves sick with the very drugs that we take to try to get us well. We don't stop to think that with proper care of our immune system we could get over most illness by ourselves.

Let me give you a quick illustration of how much we are exposed to the powerful influence of the pharmaceutical industry. The other night, I was watching a prime time television show and counted five ads for drugs for different conditions within a half-hour period! Don't think this doesn't penetrate your subconscious mind and make you reach for a pill every time you have even a minor symptom.

Most patients suffering the ravages of chronic systemic candidiasis are women. One of the reasons for this is the uniqueness of a woman's hormone system. During a portion of the menstrual cycle, progesterone is produced. This hormone creates a favorable environment for the growth of yeast in the presence of a weakened immune system. That is one reason candida problems are more prevalent in women around menstrual period time and among those taking birth control pills. I would estimate that the candida problem affects women about eight to one over men. This doesn't mean that it is unimportant to men even though they don't have it. They are greatly affected indirectly by the devastation it can create in the family when the wife and mother is experiencing a myriad of symptoms, making the round of doctors and clinics, and being been told that there is nothing wrong with her or that she should see a psychiatrist!

One of the reasons the medical profession generally fails to recognize this condition is that they were never taught in medical school that there was such a systemic problem which could cause so many symptoms in one person. Another reason may be that there wasn't so much of it around twenty or thirty years ago when many doctors were getting their education. Many of these potent drugs which cause the problem were not yet known.

Chronic Systemic Candidiasis

Systemic candidiasis usually starts in people who eat a lot of sugar foods because sugar is the food on which yeast thrive. Many times the disease begins in teen years in patients who have been treated for acne for extended periods of time with antibiotics. Sometimes it begins with a period of hospitalization for an infection or surgery during which time the medications and the additional stress compromised an otherwise healthy immune system. No matter how it starts, the progress is manifest by a gradually increasing feeling of fatigue and "just not feeling well." Periods of weakness and depression and possibly crying begin to occur for no apparent reason. Headaches or aches and pains over the body become more and more frequent. Mental confusion and forgetfulness becomes a common problem. The menstrual cycle may become altered and painful. Many times, repeated vaginal infections are "cured" with local applications of medications only to recur and be treated again. Family relations are strained because the patient is not able to cope with usual situations, and a couple's sex life "goes out the window." This is a common description of the problem, but it varies from patient to patient.

Treatment is really quite simple, (as it is with most health problems) but it can be quite prolonged. The patient must be convinced that in spite of all the negativism experienced in past treatment, there is hope of recovery. Although there are many "cookbook" measures anyone can do to improve, there are many things that are best treated individually by someone experienced in nutritional medicine.

Since sugar feeds yeast, sugar must be eliminated from the diet as nearly as possible. This means no more candy, soft drinks, cake, pie, cookies, or desserts (diet or regular). All milk and cheese must be eliminated, because they readily ferment and form yeast. All fermented products like wine, beer, and vinegar must go also for the same reasons. Adequate rest is very important. Normalization of the digestive system is extremely important because many of these patients have constipation, diarrhea, or both at times. An adequate and nutritious diet must be prescribed and conscientiously followed. Sometimes, yeast-killing prescriptions are necessary for several months. Adequate amounts of certain vitamins and minerals are necessary to enhance the recovery of the body's compromised immune system. Replacing the normal bowel bacteria (acidophilus) is also necessary. When such measures are followed, the patient begins to recover and life again becomes a pleasurable experience for both the patient and the family. One of the first signs of recovery of a married woman is when the husband notices improvement.

One of the most satisfying experiences I have as a physician is when I help a patient, whose life has been devastated, return again to being a normal and happy human being. There is hope as long as there is life and the will to get well.

The best things in life are still not "things." Have you ever paused to consider what a wonderful thing it is to be able to think? *We take it for granted. We don't understand how thought is generated or how it is retained, but we can still use the process and hopefully be blessed by it if we develop good thinking habits. It is just another of the unfathomable gifts we have been given to use even though we don't know how it works. We do know that our brains are much more efficient than the most advanced computer and have much more capacity. However, it is estimated that the average person uses less than 10 percent of the brain's thinking capacity! How much of the time we let the media do most of our thinking for us!*

How much are we being influenced by the liberal images that are brought into our homes every day on television? If we are not very careful, we will find that without thinking, we begin to accept or at least tolerate the insidious immorality being portrayed on the screen and that gradually, without thinking, we become the silent spectator watching our country "go down the tube" because we are not thinking for ourselves! Customs may change, but if we are to regain a semblance of civilization in this country, we cannot disregard the basic values and traditions that come from a belief in God and His teachings.

Most people think of "daydreaming" as a waste of time. I am not convinced this is true. Did you ever stop to think that when you daydream you always think of pleasant things, not unpleasant things? These are times when you are at peace with yourself. When you have time to relax and think about all the beautiful things in life. Ever since I was a young man, I have daydreamed about the time when things will be "on earth as they are in heaven." When I was a young man, I believed that I might see that day in my lifetime. Well, if I do, it had better get a move on. But, I can still daydream about it. I think that some of the most productive times in my life have been times when daydreaming helped me visualize my goals and helped me to pursue them. I know that daydreaming can be overdone, but for me it is a short period of total mental relaxation when I can observe and commune with nature and "charge my battery" for future activity.

At this moment, as dusk is settling over this panorama of wooded mountain beauty, the greed and hatred that is so rampant in the world today seems very far away. I think that such times of quiet and relaxation are absolutely essential if we are to maintain a worthy perspective of how beautiful life can be.

I hope that some of these aesthetic thoughts will stay with you as you pursue the more mundane subject ahead. The problem and its solution is probably not one which you would choose to discuss at your social gatherings or your bridge party; however, it is a very common problem which is the basis for lots of poor health. So, it is a subject about which I feel my patients should have an intelligent understanding if they are to attain and maintain good health.

22

Constipation

If I were to venture a guess based upon my own experience in treating people over the past forty-three years, I would say that more than 50 percent of the population is constipated. That statement will raise many eyebrows, I know, since most people think that if they have one bowel movement a day—no matter how little or how big or how hard or how soft or how odoriferous or how nonodoriferous—they are not constipated. Nothing could be farther from the truth.

There is a general misunderstanding about what constitutes constipation. Even the medical profession places very little or no importance on the regular and complete emptying of the intestinal tract. Unless the intestinal tract is doing the job for which it was designed, the person owning that intestinal tract will be unhealthy to one degree or another.

First, let us consider the purpose of the approximately twenty-eight feet of hollow tube that makes up a very important part of the digestive system. A very cursory and somewhat simple explanation is in order. The mouth is the grinding mill of the body. Its purpose is to mechanically break foods down into a small, soft mass which prepares the food for the chemical digestive process. Without complete chewing of food, incomplete digestion naturally follows.

From the mouth, food goes down a tube about eight inches long called the esophagus. The esophagus transfers food from the mouth to the stomach. The stomach is where the first part of chemical digestion takes place. Here, the chewed food is attacked by strong stomach acids which break down the protein in the food.

The next twenty-four feet of tubing is the small intestine. Here the natural bacteria and enzymes produced by other digestive organs complete the digestion of the protein foods and begins and finishes the digestion of fats and carbohydrate foods. The small intestine absorbs nutrients from foods. Keep in mind that natural bacteria have a large part to play in the utilization of our foods. Without them, (as when they are killed out by potent drugs and antibiotics) many bad things happen. When the small intestinal tract is inflamed or diseased for one reason or another, nutrients are not completely absorbed and the patient becomes malnourished in the presence of plenty. This situation is very common in today's population. The really miraculous thing about it is how people survive at all considering the terrible foods they eat and the drugs they take.

The last three feet of the bowel is called the colon. To put it bluntly, this is where the garbage is stored until it is eliminated. This part of the bowel is larger in diameter than the rest of the intestine since it has a lot of waste to hold. Although some absorption takes place in the colon, that is not its principle purpose. Strong circular muscles around the colon propel the garbage to the rectum, which is the last several inches of the intestinal tract. It is from the rectum that the utilized food is expelled as stool.

The total transit time of the food from the time it is placed in your mouth until it is eliminated as stool should be twenty-four hours! Not a lot of people accomplish this goal. What's the difference? It makes a lot of difference for several reasons. A reflex activates the proper emptying of the stomach when the bowels move. If this doesn't happen, the first step toward digestive problems and ill health has already taken place. The acids held too long in the stomach can cause gastritis and ulcers. When the garbage is kept in the colon too long, decay occurs with the consequent formation of gas which leads to bloating and discomfort. You know what happens when you leave organic material in your garbage can too long. Well, the same thing happens to it in the colon. It begins to stink. The resulting toxic gases are absorbed through the walls of the colon into the blood stream and recycled throughout the body. Not a pleasant thought. This places an overload on the other excretory organs of the body—the lungs, kidneys, and skin. As a result, the exhaled breath can have a bad odor, the pores of the skin exude irritating and foul-smelling perspiration, and the urine becomes very strong.

Constipation is the principle cause of diverticulosis and diverticulitis since the back pressure caused by the uneliminated gas puts abnormal internal pressure on the walls of the colon and bulges result. Equate this to a weak spot in an inner tube when it is inflated too much. Hemorrhoids are a direct result of constipation. When the stool is hard and large, the pressure on the walls of the rectum impairs the return blood circulation from the veins in the rectal wall and they become dilated. That is what hemorrhoids are—bulging veins in the rectum. Constipation can be a participating factor in almost any of the diseases of the body because of the toxemia it causes.

Okay, so you're constipated. What do we do now? When a chronically ill person comes into my office for care, one of the first things I have to accomplish if I am to be successful in guiding that patient back to health is to correct constipation and restore the integrity of the digestive system. The first step is to eliminate refined and processed foods from the diet since these foods have little nutrition. If you have read the preceding chapters, you know what those foods are.

Next, you must eat an adequate amount of the nutritious foods that are the key to health. You should also know what these are. The diet should emphasize fiber and bulk foods such as raw vegetables, raw fruits, nuts, whole grain breads, and cereals. These are the foods that make the bowel work, and work it must do to overcome constipation. Do not neglect adequate amounts of good protein foods such as eggs, liver, chicken, fish, beef, lamb, and cheese and all the natural foods that have been so unjustifiably denounced by the medical profession and the food manufacturers. Stay away from highly advertised pasteurized milk, artificial eggs, low-fat this and low-fat that, margarine, any "light" or "diet" foods, and heated or refined oils. These junk foods are ruining us! Pick your foods from the perimeter aisles of the grocery store, and then go home!

You must drink adequate amounts of water to keep the contents of the bowel moist and soft. It may be necessary to add more roughage to your diet for a while in the form of bran. Also, a little trick to aid your digestion is to refrain from drinking liquids while you are eating. Fluids dilute the digestive juices and impair their power to break down the food into a form that can be absorbed.

Don't expect to overcome the constipation habit overnight. It takes several weeks to several months sometimes to break the bowel of its lazy habits. But it definitely can be done, and it must be done if you are to enjoy optimum health.

I am sitting on the same deck of the same mountain retreat and looking at the same beautiful mountain site as I did when I first started writing "Letters to My Patients." Only time has changed. It is a cool 35 degrees, and it has been raining and snowing lightly for the past four hours. The cold has induced me to set up my equipment inside and observe the beauty of the countryside from in front of the fireplace.

As I start writing, I see a deer with her little fawn grazing on some of the clover in the yard that they haven't quite finished off yet. The stereo is playing the soft strains of Ed Ames singing "My Cup Runneth Over With Love"—and that is the emotion I feel at this time while I listen to the words: "In only a moment we both will be old, we won't even notice the world turning cold, and so in this moment with sunlight above, My Cup Runneth Over With Love." Those of you who have truly enjoyed life and who are perhaps in the years when there is a whole lot more life behind you than ahead of you may appreciate some of the thoughts that are running through my mind at this moment as I wax a little sentimental and feel a little moisture coming to my eyes. Where have all the years gone? It seems like only yesterday when I first fell in love with my wonderful wife. Then came our wedding. Then the children started coming—all five of those dear, wonderful people. Then the grandchildren and the great grandchildren. The struggles and the hardships and the victories. The regrets for hurts that I have at times caused those I love the most. I am sure you all have had that experience. As time becomes such a precious commodity, I wonder if those I love know how much I love them? I wonder if I have done the best I could considering the circumstances or whether there were more things I could have done, not only for my family but for those people who have entrusted me with their health and their lives. I guess there are many things in this life that we will never know.

I ramble a lot when I write. I write what I feel to help you understand what motivates me, thereby allowing you to see more clearly why I feel some of the things I express can be important to your health and enjoyment of life. Hopefully, there will be enough good thoughts to stimulate your curiosity and maybe induce you to do the things that will enhance your joy of living.

23

Intestinal Disorders

Most intestinal "diseases" are only symptoms which have been given awe-inspiring names by the medical profession so that the absence of a satisfactory treatment will be excused by the public. The three I will discuss in this chapter are irritable bowel syndrome, colitis, and ulcerative colitis. These conditions are all problems with the intestinal system (small intestine and colon). Each subsequent name indicates the same problem but in a more advanced stage of severity. The suffix "itis" merely means inflammation. Irritable bowel syndrome indicates a disturbance of the digestive system which is not yet bad enough to call an "itis" but which is causing problems. The next stage is where a detectable inflammation of the colon exists. This is called "colitis" or inflammation of the colon. The third stage is still more severe and is accompanied by not only inflammation of the lining of the colon but also mucous membrane ulcerations—hence the name ulcerative colitis.

These conditions are very common today because of our immodest and harmful lifestyles which include poor diets. Orthodox medicine seems to look upon these conditions as abnormalities which just happen to some unfortunate people and are probably brought on by stress and disease bacteria. (Almost everything that we don't really understand is usually attributed to either stress or viruses.) In my experience, these conditions are easily and successfully treated if a little attention is given to determine what the patient is doing that is actually causing nature to rebel in this particular area of the body. Things like this don't "just happen." There is always a logical explanation if we will only take the necessary time to question the patient and determine which of the rules of good health he or she is breaking. These problems are found much more frequently in females, and I don't have an explanation for that.

The longer the condition has existed, the farther it has progressed, and the more difficult and time-consuming it is to cure. However, it can usually be cured—not just symptomatically relieved until the next attack. Most of the patients I see have suffered for years and have undergone medical treatment all that time. They exhibit symptoms from just a moderate discomfort with a lot of gas and indigestion (irritable bowel syndrome) to the more serious symptoms such as severe pain, diarrhea, weight loss, and bloody stools (ulcerative colitis).

In my estimation and experience, the treatment for these conditions is quite simple. Many times the cause is the overuse of antibiotics which have sterilized the bowel. Irritation and poor absorption of nutrients result which cause malnutrition. Poor nutrition is usually the basic cause of these problems in spite of the fact that medical science refuses to consider or investigate the possibility that refined foods such as white sugar and white flour could be a factor. They also refuse to consider the use of certain vitamins and minerals in larger doses than the RDA as being curative or having any place in treatment. Those of us who have been doing nutritional work for years *know* the value of such therapy.

Most of the colon problems that have advanced to the stage of ulcerative colitis have been overtreated with antibiotics and cortisone to the point where the protective effect of the normal bacteria in the bowel has been eliminated and yeast (candida) have been allowed to invade the tissues of the digestive tract. When the yeast problem is eliminated, and the diet is corrected, and the proper vitamins and minerals are prescribed, the patient begins to recover. Recovery can be complete in a few weeks to several months, depending on the severity of the condition and the cooperation of the patient.

Treatment starts with an analysis of the patient's diet to see what he or she is eating to irritate the intestine and/or what is not being eaten that is causing a deficiency of things that are necessary to institute healing. I have found the most offending foods to be the refined flour and refined sugar products. Breaking it down a little further, I would say that soft drinks are one of the greatest offending factors. Excessive intake of pasteurized milk is also frequently a factor. A history of constipation is frequently found preceding the diagnosis of these conditions.

Vitamin and mineral supplementation is also of utmost importance. The antioxidant vitamins, particularly vitamins A, C, and E are necessary in much larger doses than the RDA. Zinc is absolutely imperative for healing the intestine. Zinc is necessary for the healing of all wounds. I call zinc "nature's healing mineral." The establishment of the normal bowel flora is of utmost importance. I use the B vitamins and acidophilus for this purpose. For the first few weeks or months of treatment, it is often necessary to use pancreatic digestive enzymes to help the patient properly metabolize their foods.

Naturally, I can't propose a general treatment plan which would work for all patients since a much more individualized approach is necessary, and self-treatment beyond the measures outlined above would not be wise. Suffice to say that most of these colitis conditions can be corrected without taking drugs for the "rest of your life" as some patients have been told. There is definitely a better way.

When I sit down to write, I think of so many things that I want to tell you which will be of practical benefit to your good mental and physical health. In my way of thinking, the two are an inseparable composite which make us the beings that we are. Don't skip over this thought lightly—read that sentence again and think about it. One aspect of health is completely dependent on the other. You may have noticed that almost all of my chapters begin with something of beauty. Hopefully, that will begin to generate the type of body chemistry which promotes good health. So, for just a little while put all negative thoughts aside and just imagine.

It is a clear and pleasant April evening in an isolated spot in the pine covered mountains. A half-moon is just setting between the silhouette of the mountain peak and the dark sky beyond. The stars are just becoming visible in the heavens, and only the soft rush of the breeze through the pine trees is audible. Just observing such majesty makes chills run up and down my spine as I contemplate the enormous amount of eternal beauty and order of the heavens. It is my belief that one day things will be the same on earth.

The best things in life are still not "things." I certainly realize this every time I hug one of my children or grandchildren or hold one of my dear little grandchildren or great grandchildren in my arms and thrill at the thought that I had some small part in helping to create that little life. We become so involved in our daily hectic efforts to struggle and win the "prize," whatever it may be, that we overlook the simpler things that make our lives really worth living. Have we acted in such a way today that we set a good example for someone who may be watching us? Have we stopped to be considerate enough to say "thank you" for a kind deed? Have we bothered to tell the ones closest and dearest to us how much we love them? Have we smiled at someone who needs the strength that a simple smile can give? Did you ever stop to think that maybe we are wasting a good part of our lives chasing things that have no permanent value while neglecting the things that really would give us fulfillment? Think about it!

24

Allergies

Allergies are a very common problem in almost all sections of the country. The definition of allergy is "an abnormal reaction to a substance." The word "abnormal" tells us that a normal body in good operating condition should not have this problem. Therefore, let us not look to some pill or shot for relief. Instead, let's try to go to the crux of the problem and find out why the body is responding in such an abnormal fashion.

The body, in perfect condition (if such a state could be found), is blessed with an immune system whose purpose is to destroy or counteract harmful substances in the environment which harm our bodies. Hence, if perfection were possible, the "policemen" circulating in our bloodstream would protect us from all harm, and we would suffer no such thing as allergies or disease of any kind. However, due to physical degeneration over the centuries and the foolish things we do to our bodies, that inherent protection has been compromised. We suffer the consequences. Genetics plays a big part in allergies because we find that people who suffer with allergies generally come from parents who suffered with allergies.

The standard medical approach to relief is to find a drug of some kind that will counteract the symptoms until the particular thing that the patient is allergic to is gone. The problem with this approach is that there isn't a medication which is so specific that it does just the job you want it to do and nothing else. There are *always* some side effects. Sometimes the side effects are more bothersome than the symptoms the drug is treating. Another, and different, approach is to inject into the body a very minute dose of the same substance (or antigen) which is causing the allergic symptoms, hoping that the body's immune system is strong enough to manufacture the necessary antibodies to destroy the antigen that is causing the problems.

This approach is more reasonable except for several variables. First, the testing methods that we have for detecting just what is causing the allergic symptoms are far from perfect, and so many times we are injecting the wrong things. Sometimes this treatment is quite satisfactory, but many times it is not. Secondly, possibly due to poor nutritional status, the body may not have the right substances present to manufacture the right antibodies. Thirdly, the many tests used in detection and the consequent treatment are so expensive that the patient may opt to suffer from the allergy!

In reality, despite the advances science has made in understanding allergies, we still know relatively little. The immune system is such a complicated protective mechanism that we may never know just how it operates. I am the first to admit that I don't know. However, even though I don't know how it works, I do know from personal knowledge I have gleaned over the years and from the experience of other practitioners under whom I have studied, that there are many things that can be done to enhance the integrity of the immune system. And, by doing these things the allergic symptoms begin to disappear. The scientific community calls this anecdotal evidence and doesn't accept it as fact. However, I am only a practicing physician, and my pragmatism tells me that if it works and doesn't hurt anybody, use it even though I can't explain how or why it works. My patients just want safe relief!

The beginning of the treatment for allergies is to quit doing the things, over which we have control, that suppress our immune systems. Hence, the first step is just that simple! Knowing what those things are is more complicated. Let's start with what seems to me to be reasonable assumptions. The human animal was made with the need for certain chemicals (food substances) with which to nourish the body. One would suspect that in the orderly nature of things, those substances should be found in things that are grown or raised. It would also seem logical to me that if those food substances were altered or added to in such a way as to make some of the necessary elements needed for the body's nutrition unavailable, then the body would not be able to operate properly.

Now I admit that this is a rather simplistic explanation and not 100% accurate, because the body is such a wonderful piece of machinery that it can manufacture within itself some of the missing nutritional elements even though we do not supply them directly in our food. It can, however, only do so much. The abuse we give it with all the tasty but nutritionally deprived foods we put in our mouths, eventually (sometimes sooner and sometimes later) takes its toll, and the body begins to break down in the areas where genetics has made us the most susceptible. Simple, if not scientific logic.

Now, down to specifics. I used to say that the two most devastating foods we eat are refined sugar and refined flour, but now I add to that list altered fats. Almost everything that we eat in a package or a can contains either refined sugar, refined flour, or some kind of altered or partially hydrogenated fat. And, these foods are deficient in the nutrition they are supposed to provide. The so-called "diet foods" are another typical example of making money at the expense of the public's health. Refined sugar has *absolutely no food value*—only calories. Refined flour has had a very large percentage of the vitamins and minerals removed from it that are supposed to nourish our bodies. The altered and partially hydrogenated fats that are everywhere in our foods cannot be properly utilized by the body, which was made to handle only natural fats. Many people with allergies would respond favorably if nothing else was done except eliminating these foods from their diets. One of the things I sometimes tell my patients is that if God made it, eat it; if man made it, don't. Obviously, this is oversimplified, but you get the idea.

We do many other things to suppress our immune systems. Many different drugs are greatly overused, especially painkillers and antibiotics. They can have a devastating effect on the immune system. Some of the most common health problems that I see in my office these days are the direct result of the repeated and unwise use of antibiotics. The basic problem is the suppression of the immune system, which manifests itself in many different ways—including allergies.

To strengthen the immune system and help allergies you *must* alter your lifestyle and/or your diet. The adrenal gland is a key gland in the immune process, and vitamin C is found more abundantly in this organ than anywhere in the body. Hence, an adequate supply of vitamin C is essential to the treatment of allergies. The key word here is "adequate." The RDA is ridiculously small. Dr. Linus Pauling, who did extensive research on vitamin C, died in 1994, but the Institute which he established carries on. Dr. Pauling taught that 2,000 mg. daily for the average person is a minimum. I take about 4,000 to 5,000 mg. per day and have for years. Dr. Pauling took 18,000 mg. per day for at least the last twenty-five years or so of his life, and he was active until his death at age ninety-three. I am certainly not recommending to any reader that he or she should take this much but only relate these amounts to impress upon you that most of the scare tactics you hear about vitamin C just have no basis in fact. Vitamin C is an important part of the treatment for allergies.

Dr. Roger Williams, Professor Emeritus at the University of Texas until the time of his death at age ninety-two, probably did more research on vitamins than any other person. He discovered pantothenic acid (B5) and found that it had many important uses, including a cortisone-like effect without any of the side effects of cortisone—even in large doses. This vitamin also appears to be very useful in the treatment of allergies; and I use it in fairly large doses. Adequate doses of B6 and Magnesium are also very helpful for allergic problems. As little as one tablespoon of flaxseed oil daily is also very effective.

It is difficult to just pick out a few individual nutrients that are important in the treatment of this problem, because the interaction of so many nutrients is essential. The above suggestions are a guide and will be very beneficial if followed. I have treated many allergic conditions successfully with these methods. It is important to remember that allergic symptoms are merely an expression of more deeply rooted problems and that it takes time and persistence to achieve satisfactory results. You will notice that success is judged from month to month and season to season, not day by day. Don't forget to exercise! Exercise is an extremely important element for building any immune system.

Another celebration of Christ's birthday has just past. We are now looking forward to a happy and healthy New Year. Eager anticipation reigns in this house as I recall all the blessings that have been ours in the past year and looking forward to an even better year with family and friends (which includes my many patients). It is my hope that your health and happiness will be improved to some degree by the knowledge you receive from the words in this book. If I have been able in some small way to make a difference in your enjoyment of life, I will have been adequately rewarded.

It is a Christmas ritual at my house to watch the old movie "It's a Wonderful Life." I'm sure you must have seen it by this time, but if you haven't, I would strongly urge you to view it. The most meaningful part to me begins near the end when George (played by James Stewart) is in the depths of despair and depression because of some financial problems. He is contemplating suicide and remarks aloud "it would be better if I had not been born." Clarence (his guardian angel) then allows him to see what the world would have been like if he had not been born. When George sees the tremendous impact his life has had on the lives of so many others, he fully comprehends the joy of being alive and how relatively unimportant his financial problems are. Clarence says, "You have been given a great gift, George—a chance to see what the world would be like without you." Clarence later tells George: "It's strange, isn't it? Each man's life touches so many other lives, and when he isn't around it leaves an awful hole." Even though I have seen this movie many times, there are a few places during this part of the movie, that in spite of myself, I can feel a few tears of emotion. This can be a good lesson for all of us.

In order to feel like our lives have been worthwhile, all of us have to know that in some ways our lives have made a positive difference in the lives of those we have served and those with whom we have come in contact. When you get a little blue, as we all do at times, think about what a blessing you have been given. And think about how much your being alive has meant to others.

25

Asthma: A Much Misunderstood Disease

Actually, when you get right down to it, asthma is really not a disease at all. It is merely a symptom—a symptom of a much deeper problem. Dr. Emanuel Cheraskin, who has been a much admired mentor of mine for several years, once wrote a paper called "The Name Of The Game Is The Name." In this paper he showed how ridiculous, but apparently paramount, it is to the medical profession to have a name for every symptom or group of symptoms. In the thinking of medicine today, without the name of the condition (diagnosis), treatment would be impossible since all treatment is based on the name of the disease. Without the name of the disease, the doctor could not go to his or her drug book to find the proper drug for the treatment of that condition. Once the disease has been named, the doctor feels that most of his work has been done since the diagnosis has been made. It is then but a simple matter to look in the book and find the recommended drug treatment.

The problem with this type of thinking is that it infers that once a diagnosis is made, a satisfactory drug treatment is available, which is definitely not the case. According to conventional thinking, when we compartmentalize the body we can also compartmentalize disease. Hence, if we have symptoms related to the heart, we can say that a patient has heart disease. Within the framework of heart disease, there are probably fifty different symptoms that are named different diseases, each of which has a particular drug which will supposedly alleviate the problem. Were it only that simple! The same thing is true of symptoms of any organ of the body. There are many symptoms referred to as kidney disease, many are referred to as ovarian disease, many that are called prostate disease, and many that are lung disease. The physician gets a great sense of pride in having put a name on the condition, but from a holistic viewpoint, this is probably a very small part of getting the patient well. It is at this point that the patient begins to suffer because medical thinking goes little deeper than the diagnosis. In my way of thinking, the real challenge for the physician just begins at this point. Now we must find out why this patient's body has responded the way it has to cause the particular symptoms which brought him or her to see us in the first place.

Dr. Roger Williams, a famous biochemist, taught us that the clinical response of each individual is different. Analyzing the lifestyle of the patient and working out the best treatment for this particular individual becomes the most difficult part of the equation. Dr. Williams called this concept "biochemical individuality." Because of genetic influence, environmental deterioration, or any number of other reasons, no two people's bodies require the same amount of any nutrient. One patient may seem to get along well on the RDA of a particular vitamin or mineral, and another person may need fifty or more times that amount just to survive. While this premise has never been accepted by orthodox medicine, it certainly has been proven to alleviate many different conditions.

Now let's get back to asthma. It is perfectly possible that thousands of dollars can be spent on laboratory work, blood tests, X-rays, magnetic resonance imaging (MRI), and breathing tests in order to arrive at this name (diagnosis) for this particular group of symptoms. It is also conceivable that with much less laboratory testing and a little more thought, the same diagnosis could have been made.

Now we come down to what I consider some of the antiquated medical thinking of our day. How many times I have heard patients say: "I'd be very healthy it wasn't for my asthma." Or, "I'd be perfectly healthy if it wasn't for my arthritis." Or, "I've been perfectly healthy all my life until this kidney disease hit me." This type of thinking infers that it is possible to have an unhealthy lung in the presence of a healthy body. It should occur to a reasonably thinking person, particularly a doctor, that there must be an underlying reason why this patient's lungs are acting the way they are. That underlying reason for the lung problem also must be affecting all other parts of the body.

It is inconceivable to think that the body's "compartments" are so isolated one from another that what affects one part has no effect on other parts. While this may seem ridiculous, this type of thinking permeates the entire medical profession. That is the reason we have specialists. Each specialist knows all the names that can be given to any particular symptom of that particular organ. And, the specialist knows all of the drugs that are used for treatment. One of the major problems with this approach is that *all* of these drugs have side effects, and some of the side effects can be as serious as the disease being treated. If a specialist suspects that another part of the body might be involved, he or she sends the patient to another specialist. Within the profession, this is known as "ping-ponging." The thought that there might be one underlying cause for the symptoms (diseases) of various organ compartments seems too illogical to consider.

The words "asthma attack" strike fear into the minds of many patients and parents of patients. In many cases, that fear is justified. The word asthma means "without air." It can be a terrifying feeling when an attack causes a serious air hunger. Orthodox medicine believes that asthma is probably an inherited tendency that is triggered by allergic responses to many different things. It just happens to some people in the same way that some people just happen to get colds or just happen to get cancer or just happen to get arthritis or any number of other conditions. In my opinion, "happenstance" has very little to do with it. In most cases, an underlying cause can be discovered, which when corrected will alleviate the particular symptoms or disease. This is called a "cure." However, the cure will only last as long as the patient's adherence to the basic principles of health which "cured" the disease in the first place. Future violations of these good health principles will again result in a recurrence of the symptoms.

The lung is composed of millions of very small tubes called bronchioles. Under normal conditions, these bronchioles have the capacity to expand as we inhale air and contract as we exhale air. During this process, the various gases in the air, including oxygen, are passed through the cell membrane into the blood stream. It is through this method that the various gases of the body are exchanged into and out of the blood stream. Of course, this is a very oversimplified description of a very complicated metabolic process. If a condition occurs which does not permit a free exchange of air into and out of the bronchioles, interference with this metabolic process occurs, and air hunger is the result. Asthma attacks occur when for some reason the muscular element in the bronchioles contract abnormally (spasm), thereby inhibiting a free exchange of an adequate amount of air.

The crisis phase of an illness is a very inefficient time for treatment as far as the basic cause is concerned. The ideal time to treat asthma is when the patient is not having an asthma attack. Current thinking prompts the doctor to only treat asthma when the patient is having trouble breathing. This is deemed treatment. Why treat a disease when the symptoms are not present? The answer to that question is quite logical. The basic cause of the disease is still present. If properly treated, the intensity and frequency of future attacks will lessen and in time probably stop them altogether. During an attack, it is, of course, necessary to temporarily utilize the standard medications for the well-being of the patient. However, treatment should not be directed only toward the temporary alleviation of symptoms but to the eradication of the basic problem.

The root cause of asthma, as with most diseases, is the ineffective functioning of the immune system. We must then ask what is the cause of the poorly functioning immune system? Here starts the detective work and the investigation of the patient's living habits and lifestyle which usually will expose a cause or many causes for the body's malfunctioning. We must first start with one of the basic considerations of any health problem. What are you putting into your mouth to nourish your body? What is the patient eating that may cause an allergic response, or what is the patient not eating which is necessary for the maintenance of a healthy body and a healthy lung?

Other than dietary considerations, many other lifestyle habits should be studied. Do you smoke? Do you get adequate exercise? Are you constipated? Are you working around harmful fumes or chemicals that could be irritating to the lungs? Another factor osteopathic physicians should consider is the proper structural integrity of the bony and muscular systems of the body, particularly in the area of the spine from which the nervous enervation of the lungs originates. So, I find that osteopathic manipulative therapy is very important also. Many or all of the above factors should be corrected if the cause of asthma is to be overcome.

Now, to be a little more specific about some of the things that can be done to start the rebuilding of the integrity of the immune system in order to eventually overcome asthma. Please be advised that I am not advocating that asthma medications be stopped immediately, although that is certainly the ultimate goal. As the patient gets better and better, these medications are gradually eliminated. In my forty-three years of medical experience, I have found that there are certain generalizations that I can make about all asthmatics. These do not necessarily agree with prevailing medical opinion. Asthmatics do not tolerate cow's milk in any form. Most asthmatics have a calcium, phosphorus, and magnesium imbalance due to the ingestion of refined sugar and soft drinks—diet or regular, it makes no difference. Soft drinks contain significant amounts of phosphoric acid as a preservative. This upsets the normal calcium, phosphorus, and magnesium ratio in the blood. In turn, this imbalance causes bronchial tubes to contract and spasm. This is called asthma. There can also be an allergic action to many of the preservatives and dyes. Unfortunately, many of these mineral imbalances do not show up in standard laboratory blood testing.

Almost all asthmatics are magnesium deficient and have a relative overabundance of calcium. If you are to understand the relationship between the muscular spasm of the bronchial tubes and calcium and magnesium, a brief explanation is in order. Calcium is a mineral which is overpublicized, and the need for it is accepted. However, magnesium is a mineral about which the public knows very little. But, it is a mineral that is absolutely necessary for the proper utilization of calcium. In order for calcium to pass in and out of the muscle cells, magnesium *must be present* in adequate amounts.

Most people believe wrongly that calcium relaxes muscles. Calcium is the mineral which adds tone to the muscle. When present in more than normal amounts, it causes muscular spasm. Magnesium causes muscle relaxation, and if present in adequate amounts, prevents the muscle spasm. Hence, magnesium must be present in the muscle cells of the bronchial tree to help prevent the bronchial spasm. All of this may seem rather complicated, but it really isn't. A step in the right direction is to stop eating the refined flour foods because the refining process removes most of the magnesium. Of course, anyone with half a brain should know that smoking and asthma are incompatible.

Because of inadequate nutrition over a prolonged period of time, most asthmatics need vitamin and mineral supplementation. While it is impossible in a book such as this to prescribe specific doses, certain generalizations can be drawn. For anyone over 70 or 80 pounds, 500 to 600 mg. of magnesium daily in at least two divided doses is generally well tolerated. Remember, however, that magnesium has a laxative effect. If taken in more than adequate quantities, it can cause diarrhea. In certain cases, much more than 600 mg. is necessary. Vitamin A is very essential to the cellular lining of the bronchial tubes and is many times deficient in asthmatics. Adults can safely take 25,000 units of natural vitamin A in the form of fish liver oil capsules without fear of overdose.

The glucose metabolism of most asthmatics usually has been impaired due to the ingestion of too much refined sugar. The vitamin B complex is necessary for proper carbohydrate metabolism and energy production. I generally recommend a B complex which contains about 50 mg. of all the B factors. Since vitamin B is water soluble, there is no danger of overdose in these quantities. It will, however, make the urine a very bright yellow as some of the B2 (riboflavin) passes through the kidney. Vitamin C is another very essential nutrient supplement. It is one of the most potent antioxidants, and is necessary for detoxification and in strengthening the immune system. I generally have most of my adult patients take at least 3,000 mg. daily in divided doses. I would advise patients with asthma problems who have been unsuccessful in finding relief to seek the services of a qualified, nutritionally oriented physician.

It's a blustery Saturday afternoon in Alto. The wind is blowing hard, and the tall pines are bending as I look out toward the snow-covered Sierra Blanca peak. The temperature is about 37 degrees, but the wind has driven me inside to my writing spot in the loft.

There is a picture hanging in one of my treating rooms that draws a lot of comment from my patients. My youngest daughter gave it to me many years ago, and I value it highly because of the sentiment it portrays. The picture is of an old, weather-beaten cowboy sitting on an old box fixing a saddle. The inscription under the picture is: "It's not near as important how many years a fellow has lived as how many other folks have been right glad he has." If we would all try to live in such a way that after we are gone people would think of us in that light, this old world would be a far better place.

As I sit here in the loft today as mother nature is expressing her authority and power outside, I am letting my thoughts wander. When I think of the old cowboy in the picture, I think of the many people who have had a strong, positive influence on my life. Many of them are gone now. As I get older, I realize how important it is to let those who are still around know how much they are appreciated. Such an opportunity missed may never come again.

We see so much hatred, strife, and cruelty in the world today. It is impossible to escape because the news media seems to find nothing else to write about, and television and movie producers can find little but trash to bring into our homes. The fault, however, is with us. We don't have to watch the programs that offend our sensitivities. Until we stop watching and reading such junk, the media will continue to put it there. When their profit margin disappears and the bottom line turns to red, it will cease.

I think it does our inner beings good to occasionally spend a little time thinking about the deeper feelings within us—to think about how our actions influence others and how we can pass on some of God's blessings. I remember when I was just a teenager (and that requires a good memory), my mother and dad used to listen to a gospel singer almost every morning. I don't remember his name, but I do remember the words to the song he always sang to open the program. I think they are quite appropriate to this kind of sentimental thinking. "If I have wounded any soul today, if I have caused one foot to go astray, if I have sinned in my own willful way, dear Lord, forgive." What a beautiful thought.

26

Acne: The Teenager's Nightmare

Puberty is a time of varying degrees of psychological trauma to the teenager. It is a time when childhood has not quite been outgrown and adulthood is just slightly out of grasp. It is a time when bodily hormone changes initiate physical development characteristics with which the teenager is not yet comfortable. It is a "between" time of personality and behavioral uncertainty. It is a time when physical appearance is of paramount importance and when any observable imperfection is imagined to be unacceptable to peers. What a time for *acne* to rear its ugly head! I have seen many young people isolate themselves from normal youth activities because they were so self-conscious about the appearance of their skin.

Orthodox dermatology considers acne to be a "skin problem" and therefore only treats the skin. The usual treatment is topical drying creams, cortisone creams, and antibiotic creams. When this doesn't work well enough, oral antibiotics are given for long periods of time. This frequently creates other problems. The patient with severe acne is frequently given extremely potent and dangerous drugs by the doctor who is never willing to admit that the problem is one of the body as well as the skin and that the skin is only a mirror reflecting deeper bodily disturbances. Very few dermatologists ever consider that the patient's poor eating habits and lifestyle could be the real cause of the skin eruptions. I have seen many young people with acne who had been to many doctors. None of these youths had ever been questioned about what they ate or about their elimination habits.

The skin is a very important organ of the body. It is not just a wrapping to hold the body together. It has many functions; one of the most important functions is the elimination of waste and toxic material through the pores. The skin is equally as important as the lungs, the kidneys, and the bowels for this function. Then, why does it never occur to those treating acne that the pores of the skin may be irritated and susceptible to infection because of the toxic material that is passing through them?

Teenagers are particularly at risk for several reasons. Hormone changes are occurring in the body which many times makes the skin somewhat oily. Eating habits during the teenage years are often extremely bad. Constipation is frequently a problem because of poor eating habits and the patient's reluctance to take the time for proper elimination. It is often "put off" because of more urgent activities until the bowel no longer responds to its normal stimuli.

Acne is generally a very simple and rewarding thing to treat because the success rate is so high with *proper* treatment. Skin health comes from within—not from without. The most difficult part of treating acne in teenagers is getting them to resist the temptations of following the eating and drinking habits of their peers! Once that hurdle is overcome, the rest is relatively easy and satisfying results can be obtained.

One of the most important facets of treatment is establishing normal elimination habits. The bowels must move fully, easily, and completely at least once a day and preferably more. This is accomplished by increasing the fiber content of the diet with lots of vegetable salads, fresh fruit, whole grain breads and cereals, and sometimes raw bran flakes.

Next, the non-nutritious "junk" foods must be eliminated from the diet. From my experience, soft drinks (diet or regular—they are equally harmful) and concentrated sugar "treats" like candy, cake, cookies, chocolate, and ice cream are the main dietary factors which cause the subsequent nutritional deficiencies.

The next step is to provide the skin with the nutrients it needs to make and keep it healthy. It does very little good to try to "cop out" by taking the necessary supplements without stopping the offending junk foods. The silver bullets that help skin are *natural* vitamin A and zinc. If I were going to use only two supplements, they would be vitamin A and zinc. Large doses of vitamin A are sometimes necessary.

I know you hear about the danger of taking vitamin A because of potential toxicity, but I believe that to be largely scare tactics. I have only seen about three cases of vitamin A toxicity in my entire practice life, and they corrected themselves within a couple of weeks after stopping the excessive intake. Synthetic vitamin A is usually the culprit that causes toxicity. The body seems to have no problem with natural vitamin A obtained from fish liver oil.

Under my supervision, I generally start patients out with between 50,000 and 100,000 units of vitamin A daily for a month or so. Then, I check the patient to make sure the dose was satisfactory. By that time, considerable healing has taken place and the dose is generally lowered.

I don't believe anyone has ever died from vitamin A toxicity. Yet, to hear about it on television, you would think that it was killing as many people as some of the dangerous drugs the FDA approves for indiscriminate use. Varying estimates of up to 150,000 deaths a year from prescription drugs seem to receive no attention in the media.

Patients are generally started at 100 mg. of zinc daily for a month and then adjusted under supervision. It is certainly necessary to have adequate amounts of some of the other vitamins, minerals, and fatty acids that are good for the skin. I sometimes prescribe a tablespoon of flaxseed oil taken by mouth daily.

One particular patient stands out in my memory when I think of the dreadful personality problems that can arise from severe acne. Several years ago, a very shy and self-conscious twenty-two year old unmarried woman came into my office for treatment of severe acne. Her otherwise attractive face was covered with large infected areas of abscess, resulting in extremely unattractive skin. I could tell by her demeanor that her appearance had ruined her social life and that she had hidden herself from society. She didn't date or participate in the usual activities of young people.

She had been treated for several years by many different dermatologists by the usual methods with unsatisfactory results and, actually, with very detrimental effects. She had been on antibiotics constantly for several years. I treated this young lady for about four or five months. Her treatment was a little more complicated than I described above because she had several other problems which had been induced by the drugs and the treatment she had received (this is called iatrogenic illness—doctor induced). She was gradually taken off her medications while being treated nutritionally. At the end of the few months of treatment, she didn't have a blemish on her face, and her personality had completely changed. She was dating and having fun, and her true personality had emerged from behind the wall of self-consciousness. What a rewarding experience for me. I still have her "before" and "after" pictures, and it makes me feel good every time I look at them. I wish I could help all of my patients with their various problems as much as I was able to help her.

I sit watching the billowing white clouds move across the sky in incessant waves, at times obscuring the mountain peaks in the distance and then moving on as if drawn by a huge magnet. Peace and tranquility seem to pervade the atmosphere, and I feel at peace with my God and His creations. What a wonderful feeling. How very much the practice of such tranquility enhances our physical health and joy of living! As I have told you before (and I repeat it frequently because it is so important), such periods of inner peace produce measurable chemistry within our bodies which assists the promotion of good health. Hence, a double benefit: a wonderful feeling and the enhancement of good health!

I am thinking at this time of a lovely patient whose name shall remain a secret. Many of her health problems are due to the tensions which she creates for herself. If there is nothing really to worry about, she can find something. The frustrations are exhibited in physical symptoms. But she is learning gradually how to relax and is benefiting from the relaxation.

Those who spend most of their time in the busy urban areas of large cities pursuing questionable goals, need to get up high on a mountain and take time to look at the world that God has created for us. What a happy and satisfying experience!

From the time we are teenagers, we are taught to pursue goals that we think of as success; that is as it should be.

When we achieve those goals, however, we often find that we have done so to the neglect of a much more valuable commodity—our health. What good is success if in our zeal for achievement we lose the very thing that allows us to enjoy that for which we have expended a lifetime of effort?

If I don't have good health myself, how can I be expected to teach you how to be healthy? Doctors should be in the business of selling health, but if we don't have health to sell, we are cheating our patients. People learn by example far better than by preaching. Would you follow the dictates of a preacher who taught one code of behavior on Sunday and practiced another during the week? Would you go for advice on how to have a happy marriage to a newspaper columnist whose personal life was in shambles? Likewise, would you go to a doctor who has a stomach ulcer to find out how to cure your ulcer or to a doctor who is crippled with arthritis to get advice on how to help your arthritis? Common sense says no!

Those of you who are fifty-five to sixty years of age or more will probably remember the name Bernard McFadden. He was an enthusiastic advocate of physical culture and good nutrition. He published many articles and wrote many books about health, exercise, and proper diet. He was ridiculed by the medical profession of his day because he had no formal medical education and was hence considered "medically ignorant." Yet, the people who were doing the scoffing would have been hard pressed to accomplish any of his physical feats.

He taught by example. To celebrate his eightieth birthday, he made the headlines by performing a successful parachute jump in full view of the news cameras. He taught thousands of people how to eat and exercise successfully to attain and maintain good health, but his methods were never emulated by the health professionals. I sometimes get the idea that we in the medical profession are being outclassed by nutritionists and physical culture advocates. Maybe we should teach more by example and not practice so much with medicine!

27

Arthritis

One of the most prevalent and distressing diseases of civilization, particularly as we age, is arthritis. In this chapter, I am going to be writing about degenerative or osteoarthritis; they are one and the same. All of the causes of arthritis are probably not known, and orthodox medicine says there is no cure for it. I will agree that if too much joint destruction has already taken place, that is probably true. Since there is no officially recognized cure, the profession's general treatment is to prescribe anti-inflammatory medicine and instruct the patient to "learn to live with it." The problem is that the medicine used to relieve the pain is very often quite destructive to the inside of the stomach and intestines. The unfortunate patient is then given other prescriptions for other medicines to try to help heal the damage caused by the first medicine. On and on it goes—great for the pharmaceutical companies, but costly and painful for the patient. There are, in my opinion and experience, much better answers.

If arthritis is a disease of aging, then I must not be getting old. Gee, that would be great, but the 74 years I have on the calendar assures me that is not the case. However, I do not have arthritis. That leads me to believe, as I have always suspected, that lifestyle has a lot to do with the acquisition of arthritis.

Although there may be hereditary reasons for arthritis, my experience confirms the fact that environmental factors have much more to do with it. Let me tell you about a typical patient with early arthritis that I treated. He was about sixty years of age and was beginning to have so much discomfort and stiffness in the joints of his hands that it was interfering with his work and his golf; that is when it began to get serious!

Examination of the patient revealed early arthritis. Joint destruction had not yet taken place, but the signs and symptoms were unmistakable. He had already sought the advice of a bone specialist who told him that there was nothing he could do about it but take aspirin or similar drugs. Evaluation of the patient's diet (which no one else had ever questioned) revealed the fact that he indulged in many refined foods, including many refined flour foods and sugar foods like candy, pie, cake, soft drinks, spaghetti, white bread, and ice cream. I explained to him that ingestion of refined sugar depletes the body of the vitamin B complex because it takes a lot of vitamin B to help metabolize sugar.

Vitamin B is absolutely essential to the utilization of magnesium which, in turn, is necessary for the utilization of calcium, which in turn, is necessary for healthy joint function. It is interesting to note how much each nutrient depends on another, and when any serious single deficiency develops, it causes health to tumble like a row of dominos. The phosphoric acid found in soft drinks is very destructive to the normal and delicate calcium-phosphorous ratio in the body. That also leads to improper calcium metabolism.

This patient changed his diet radically. He ate more raw fruits and vegetables and no more refined flour or sugar foods.

He also started taking some of the vitamins and minerals and other supplements that I prescribed for him. Within two months, this patient was working and playing golf without any discomfort. The stiffness in the fingers and hands had completely disappeared. This was one of the easier cases because the disease had not progressed to the point of obvious joint destruction. They are not always this easy. But even in the more advanced cases satisfying improvement can be made *if* the patient is willing to use some will power and make the necessary alterations in his or her lifestyle. Lifetime habits are sometimes very difficult to change; in which case very limited improvement can be made.

Contrary to what most people think, arthritis is not caused by too much calcium, even though there is excessive buildup of calcium in the affected joint. Actually, nature draws calcium from the bones of the joint due to improper calcium metabolism, and the joint then becomes roughened and laden with calcium buildup. It requires certain vitamins, minerals, and fatty acids to properly utilize calcium. If we constantly eat foods without adequate quantities of these things, the disease process begins and then accentuates with continued abuse.

Arthritis can be cured if it has not advanced to the point of excessive joint destruction and if the patient has the discipline to forego the previous habits that started the disease process in the first place. It is impossible for me to outline a "cookbook" program for arthritis in all patients because each patient possesses biochemical individuality and has to be evaluated according to needs. There are, however, some basic rules that apply. I will enumerate a few of them.

1. Stop eating foods made of refined flour and sugar! That means all of the goodie desserts, soft drinks, and refined breads. Don't switch to the artificial sweeteners, they are just as bad and cause other problems.

2. Stop drinking pasteurized and homogenized milk. This may sound crazy since milk is supposed to be "nature's most perfect food," but it isn't so.

3. Take adequate amounts of calcium, magnesium, zinc, and vitamin B—particularly B6. Magnesium and B6 are very important in calcium metabolism.

4. Essential Omega 3 fatty acids are very important. For arthritis, cod liver oil is preferred.

5. Regular and complete bowel emptying is very important. Sometimes it takes a lot of attention to the digestive system in order to normalize the utilization of even good foods.

These are just a few of the major things all arthritis patients have to learn and do if they are to improve or eliminate their problem. There are more things that can be done, and they must be prescribed on an individual basis. Certainly, this is one place where "one size fits all" is not appropriate.

Well, I hope you have learned something from this chapter. If you have, I have been adequately rewarded.

My philosophy of health is quite simple. I always try to assume that if the body has the strength to stay alive, it has the strength to improve if given the proper nutrition and conditions. You have the power to help yourself if you will only assume it.

I guess I'm known to be a little bit sentimental, particularly about my family and my patients. A little moistness comes to my eyes when the right strings are pulled; so, now I'm going to see if I can pull some of yours. Most of my patients are mothers and fathers or grandmothers and grandfathers or great grandmothers and great grandfathers as are my wife and I. So, the emotions that I am going to express may strike a chord in your heart also.

Although it has been more than fifty years since the children in our family started coming, it seems like only yesterday that I held our little babies in my arms and marveled at the little creations that God had given us. What a miracle a new life demonstrates! How could the little body features be so perfect? How could the little arms and legs be so symmetrical? What would this little baby's future be? What makes it breathe? What is life anyway? So many unanswered questions. The only thing that we knew for sure was that we loved those little children.

Because I do most of my writing from my little mountain home in Alto, New Mexico, I spend a lot of time on the road. While I am driving, I have a lot of time to think and to listen to good music. I was listening to a tape on my way up here this week which brought a few tears to my eyes as I relived in my memory the sentiments and thoughts expressed in the song. Since most of you have probably also had similar experiences and feelings, I am going to tell you about it. The name of the song was "Daddy's Little Girl," sung by Al

Martino. Certainly the name of the song could just as well have been "Daddy's Little Boy." The words go like this:

"You're the end of the rainbow, my pot of gold,
You're Daddy's little girl, to have and hold,
A precious gem is what you are,
You're Mommy's bright and shining star.

You're the spirit of Christmas, my star on the tree,
You're the Easter Bunny for Mommy and me,
You're sugar and spice and everything nice and
You're Daddy's Little Girl."

That song brought back so many memories of years gone by. I can vividly remember holding our own little babies in my arms as I now hold our grandchildren and our great grandchildren. Those are feelings that should never disappear from our lives; they make us better people.

Although our children are now too big to hold in my lap, I still want to hug them as I did many years ago. I wonder why customs have made it seem inappropriate to express emotions and love just because our loved ones have gotten bigger and older? We love them just as much as ever. At what point in life does physical expression become taboo? There are people starving for love and affection as we stand back and wonder if it is appropriate for us to give them that for which they are starving. There are certain things that multiply only when given away. Certainly among those things would have to be listed love, kindness, joy, and courtesy. The more we give of these qualities to other people, the more we have to give.

There are so many beautiful things for us to think about. We all benefit from the sights and sounds and feelings of beauty. The degradation, immorality, selfishness, and violence that are ever present around us seem to cheapen life so much and bring out the worst in us. How much better it is to enrich our thinking and our hearts with thoughts of generosity and love.

28

Fibromyalgia: A Puzzling Name with a Simple Cure

Fibromyalgia is merely a complex of symptoms that orthodox medicine has given a name in order to make it seem worthy of the thousands of dollars you may spend in diagnosis and consequent treatment. I might add that the drug treatments may be entirely unsatisfactory and may cause side effects as bad as the disease.

Symptoms of fibromyalgia include generalized pain in the muscles and joints of the body, extreme fatigue, and debility due to soreness.

When you come right down to it, there is only one real disease (excluding accidents, trauma, and genetic disorders), and that is *illness*. It doesn't really matter what name you hang on it. Naming the symptoms merely makes it a lot easier to find the medicine that is supposedly going to help it. All illness, whether it be arthritis, nephritis, heart attack, ulcers, hypoglycemia, diabetes, panic attacks, chronic fatigue syndrome, fibromyalgia, or any other disease name you can think of, is ultimately just a breakdown of the body's defensive mechanism or immune system. The purpose of the doctor is to find out what the patient is doing or not doing that has caused the symptoms to become so severe that he or she comes to you for help.

Most illnesses have common causes which can be found if we just take the time to seek them out. For instance, fibromyalgia is almost always preceded, somewhere in the time frame of the previous few months, by some severe or prolonged bodily stress. Very often the apparent triggering factor is a severe case of the flu and complications which have necessitated fairly prolonged use of antibiotics. In other cases, the triggering factor may be a period of hospitalization for surgery from which the person had a difficult time recovering. There is a very gender-specific trait to fibromyalgia. The vast majority of the victims who display the symptoms of fibromyalgia are women in the younger to middle-age years.

It has been my observation over the years that each individual has certain physical weakness patterns in their body and that stresses, no matter whether those stresses are physical, mental, or nutritional, will usually affect that particular organ system of the body. In other words, from the same apparent cause, different people will develop different symptoms in different parts of the body which are called by different names. Since (as I have described in previous chapters), the name of the game is the name, each person is thought to have a different "disease" when in reality they all stem from the same cause, and the treatment for all of them should be the same. In each case, it is necessary to find the deficiency in the patient's lifestyle that has caused the "weak link" to snap and then correct it. That is what makes my job so interesting, challenging, and at times frustrating.

Dr. Roger Williams' position on biochemical individuality appears to be very important in this context because most people who are subjected to the same stresses do not fall victim to these symptoms. It is another very interesting phenomenon that some people subjected to like stresses fall victim to other symptom patterns known as arthritis, chronic fatigue syndrome, or chronic systemic candidiasis.

In the patient who develops the painful and debilitating muscular symptoms of fibromyalgia, we must address the question: "What is it that made this particular patient respond to the causative stresses with symptoms relating to the structural system of the body?" I see lots of cases of fibromyalgia and most of these cases already have been diagnosed by several different doctors as having either fibromyalgia or fibromyalgia rheumatica or fibromyositis (all are actually the same condition). All the patients have been given many different kinds of medications. The medications usually caused more side effects than the patient was willing to tolerate, and in desperation, the doctor suggests that she should visit a psychologist or a psychiatrist.

In these cases, there are usually many years of debilitating nutritional practices which weaken the patient's immune system before the final stress (the one that breaks the camel's back) takes place. However, in my experience, there is *always* a critical deficiency that rarely shows up in blood tests or laboratory analysis; that deficiency is *magnesium*. These patients rarely have only one nutritional deficiency, but I have found magnesium to be the magic and necessary bullet. However, since magnesium in therapeutic doses has a laxative effect, it is difficult if not impossible, to give enough orally to get the job done. I therefore give large doses of magnesium as well as other vitamins and minerals intravenously. Intravenously administered magnesium does not have a laxative effect. As an osteopathic physician, I have found structural manipulation a great help in restoring muscular integrity and obtaining relief of symptoms.

By the time I see patients with this "disease," they have usually had it for a long time. It does not get well overnight just because proper therapy is started. It usually takes many weeks to a few months before the patient is "cured." The relief is permanent as long as the proper lifestyle is followed.

IN RETROSPECT

It is difficult to condense the most salient knowledge that I have gained in forty-three years of my osteopathic medical practice into a little more than 200 pages. In the pages you have read, I have tried to teach you many of the simple answers to help you overcome what might appear to be many of the most perplexing health problems. While doing so, I have also tried to help you to envision a philosophy which can make your life a happier and more enjoyable experience. It has certainly worked for me.

I hope that I have been able to help you understand that many, no I would say most, of the common health problems can be overcome by diligence in pursuing some of the truths that are contained in this book. If I have been able to help you understand that most of our health problems are of our own making and that they can be corrected by reversing some of our poor lifestyle habits, then I will consider myself well rewarded. If I have been able to open your eyes to the fact that the medical profession leaves much to be desired in its treatment of the commonplace and chronic illnesses, and in fact, may be causing many of them, I will feel I have succeeded.

It is my sincere hope that from the study of the information in this book, you will gain a feeling of well-being and a perspective of life which will make living a joy.

Here's to your good health and happiness!

Index

C

T

U

NOTES

NOTES

NOTES

NOTES

NOTES

NOTES

NOTES

NOTES

NOTES

NOTES

NOTES

About the Author

Harlan O. L. Wright is an osteopathic physician, specializing in nutritional medicine. He has practiced for more than forty-three years; thirty-seven of them in Lubbock, Texas, where he lives with his wife, Lynne. Dr. Wright had five children, eleven grandchildren, and two great-grandchildren. He continues his busy practice and frequently has articles published in medical and nutritional journals. Dr. Wright pursues a vigorous lifestyle. He is a National Doubles Tennis Champion in the 70+ age group. Most of the letters compiled in this book were written from his "little piece of heaven"—his mountain home in Alto, New Mexico.

Shallowater Press
P.O. Box 1151
Shallowater, Texas 79363-1151

E-mail: SWPress@aol.com